ONLINE COUNSELLING AND GUIDANCE SKILLS

This book is accompanied by a companion website, which offers further exercises, resources and case studies. You can access these extra online materials from the *Online Counselling and Guidance Skills* webpage www.sage pub.co.uk/janeevans

'A very practical text that provides professionals new to this arena with a good introduction to what they can expect to encounter in online work. The book contains numerous thought-provoking examples and exercises for those contemplating work in virtual arenas.'

Terry Hanley, Lecturer in Counselling, University of Manchester

'Thinking about counselling online? It may seem like the best way of getting clients; *and* you can work from your home computer. Are you trained to do this? It's tempting to think that face-to-face experience translates straightforwardly to online work. But it doesn't. Jane Evans shows how many different aspects there are to counselling online. This comprehensive text is well illustrated with examples, and encourages the prospective counsellor to use well-thought-out exercises to examine just how thought out the practitioner's plans are to use this particular medium. My advice would be, don't attempt it until you have worked through this book.'

Professor Michael Jacobs, author of Psychodynamic Counselling in Action

'This practical, skills-focused book makes an important contribution to the growing literature on online counselling and guidance. It will provide a very current and valuable resource for practitioners interested in setting up and maintaining good practice online.'

Jeannie Wright, pioneer of online therapeutic practice in the UK and Associate Professor in Counselling, Massey University

ONLINE COUNSELLING AND GUIDANCE SKILLS

A Resource for Trainees and Practitioners

JANE EVANS

Los Angeles • London • New Delhi • Singapore • Washington DC

First published 2009

Apart from any fair dealing for the purposes of research or
private study, or criticism or review, as permitted under the
Copyright, Designs and Patents Act, 1988, this publication
may be reproduced, stored or transmitted in any form, or by
any means, only with the prior permission in writing of the
publishers, or in the case of reprographic reproduction, in
accordance with the terms of licences issued by the Copyright
Licensing Agency. Enquiries concerning reproduction outside
those terms should be sent to the publishers.

SAGE Publications Ltd
1 Oliver's Yard
55 City Road
London EC1Y 1SP

SAGE Publications Inc.
2455 Teller Road
Thousand Oaks, California 91320

SAGE Publications India Pvt Ltd
B 1/I 1 Mohan Cooperative Industrial Area
Mathura Road
New Delhi 110 044

SAGE Publications Asia-Pacific Pte Ltd
33 Pekin Street #02-01
Far East Square
Singapore 048763

Library of Congress Control Number: 2008924330

British Library Cataloguing in Publication data

A catalogue record for this book is available from
the British Library

ISBN 978-1-4129-4864-7
ISBN 978-1-4129-4865-4 (pbk)

Typeset by C&M Digitals (P) Ltd., Chennai, India
Printed in India by Replika Press Pvt. Ltd

CONTENTS

FOREWORD

Gary S. Stofle, LISW, LICDC, Columbus, Ohio, USA

I began providing online counselling in 1997 using a chat room in response to a request for help from a young woman who was experiencing some very significant difficulties. No books or articles existed at that time to inform my online practice; no training opportunities were available. Myself and a growing number of providers cautiously provided counselling using the computer, being mindful of potential ethical quandaries that could arise but at the same time committed to providing help to those who, for a number of distinct reasons, were unable to access therapy and counselling in a more traditional venue.

Since that time, we have learned to adapt and adjust face-to-face counselling skills into effective work online. This book acquaints the reader with that knowledge. Written as a handbook for the new counsellor as well as a reference for those more experienced, Jane Evans addresses the full continuum of issues related to online counselling from philosophy and ethics to practical, 'nuts and bolts' skills. This book is also useful to allied professionals (health providers and university/college personnel), more and more of whom are interacting with patients and students over the Internet and through email.

Jane Evans uses practical examples throughout the book to assist the reader in developing the needed skills to work successfully online. The reader can clearly see a simulated client express issues and problems through email or chat, and then see a therapeutic, empathetic response by the counsellor. Through these examples, Evans demonstrates what the research is bearing out: that a therapeutic, empathetic, healing relationship can be formed using only text.

Jane Evans also uses worksheets, exercises and assignments to help the reader learn about what is needed to do effective counselling and communicating online as well as to tune into potential issues and problems in online counselling. Significant learning about online counselling and communication can occur through active participation during the reading of this book.

Jane Evans predicts, and I agree, that online counselling and computer-related personal services will continue to grow. More and more people across the globe are 'connected' and are becoming more comfortable purchasing both goods and services over the Internet. Evans notes that the Federal Government in the United States is currently sponsoring a series of e-therapy demonstration projects for a total grant award of six million dollars divided up between four providers. This shows significant confidence in online counselling and therapy. We are consistently finding that using the computer to counsel is a viable alternative to traditional face-to-face counselling for clients. Jane Evans has written an important book that will be useful in both the initial and further training of online counsellors and other helpers.

PREFACE

The movement towards expanding online counselling, mental health, support, and guidance to clients via online computer-mediated resources is experiencing a dramatic increase. Professionals and support organisations are seeking to expand and diversify the context of their resources in a manner to accommodate the identified needs of their client groups, whilst also utilising available staffing resources and modern technology to provide the most beneficial, cost-effective services, and competitive practice. This movement is driven by the need to optimise the accessibility of support to service users, whilst also providing flexibility in the nature of technology resources which are available to assist in such spheres of practice. Providing a service or resource through online communication is convenient, as well as being easy to facilitate, as computer literacy and competency are skills that are broadly commonplace across all generations. Such flexibility and the potential for immediacy in responses to client needs can be of particular importance, specifically in the area of addiction treatments (Zelvin, 2003).

The domains of counselling, mental health, academia, and support services are particularly active in introducing a wide variety of online services for their client groups. Pergament (1998) defines online therapy as an outgrowth of four important elements within the history of psychoanalysis and psychotherapy, with particular emphasis on the work of Freud as a contributing influence. In this relatively new field of working with clients, there are publications available to practitioners that can provide a generalised insight into the practicalities of engaging with clients and offer guidance on the technology variations and requirements. There is an apparent lack of published material on a broader scale which directs trainees and practitioners in a variety of contexts requiring guidance towards the development and application of online counselling skills with their service users.

Previous published material has focused on utilising a variety of computer-mediated approaches within counselling and therapy practices without consideration being given to its potential adaptability to additional professional contexts.

This book focuses on supporting trainees and practitioners by illustrating the necessary skills required to improve service delivery in an innovative and professional manner alongside ethical considerations which are not limited to a specific area of professional practice.

Why elect to work online with service users?

Counselling skills are an integral part of everyday communication, both in a personal and professional context. They are a necessary competence for practitioners whether working in a face-to-face context or when conversing in an online environment. They are skills which are beneficial to developing relationships, whilst also enhancing the empathy, understanding, and needs of fellow human beings. In a therapeutic context, they are the essential tools required of a professional to facilitate personal growth, personal awareness, and the alleviation of the impact of mental health difficulties. *Online Counselling and Guidance Skills: A Resource for Trainees and Practitioners* offers direction in this area of work whilst also illustrating the general use of online counselling skills. This in turn may open up opportunities for other related professionals to consider where they may be able to expand their service delivery into working online with clients. Literary techniques have been successfully utilised within face-to-face therapeutic encounters since the evolution of counselling and psychotherapy practice and are also relevant to online therapy (Murphy and Mitchell, 1998).

Having competence and experience in face-to-face counselling skills does not automatically translate into holding competence in an online context without adaptation and the development of existing skills.

For some professionals, their work will lead them to a combination of face-to-face and online working with service users. An example of this might be where a client moves away from the locality but wishes to continue with accessing support for the individual or service beyond a face-to-face relationship. There might be circumstances preventing clients in having access to services due to physical restrictions, financial resources, being demographically distanced from accessing local services, personal inhibitions, and social stigma. These circumstances might arise in a wide variety of service provisions. Where it does occur, it is extremely beneficial that professionals are familiar and confident in making the transition from using face-to-face counselling skills to applying them within computer-mediated technology.

Growth in this area is further promoted by clients seeking counselling and support via an electronic medium which is accessible and can be arranged at a mutually convenient time and in the privacy of their own home. This is particularly relevant when considering current working patterns as online services can be asynchronous and planned flexibly around personal schedules. For clients who are limited in their mobility, or who have a disability which restricts their access and inclusion to face-to-face contact, the availability of online support is an invaluable resource. Seeking online support can often be a first step for those lacking in confidence or who have personal barriers in accessing a more traditional entry route to receiving personal support.

The current development is strongly influenced by a need to move the traditional focus of counselling, guidance, and support into a position where modern technology is used to provide a resource which is available and flexible in relation to accessibility for client groups and professionals who offer an online service. This is currently evident within a broad variety of counselling, health and social care, and educational contexts providing online support with availability over a 24-hour, seven days a week timespan.

I anticipate that within the next five years, the provision of online counselling and other related personal support services will be more prevalent. Interest and awareness of online working and support will continue to develop and grow. This book will provide a valuable resource for all professionals who wish to familiarise themselves with online working and who seek the option of extending their professional work to include online practice. The publication is also a useful supplementary reading and research resource for tutors and students involved in general counselling training modules and programmes, as there is currently a deficit in the subject area of online counselling being acknowledged and validated within graduate training programmes (Trepal et al., 2007). Practitioners studying at this level of qualification should be provided with insight and skills training in online counselling as this field of therapy is currently accepted as falling within the spectrum of helping relationships in a global context.

The book will also be a general interest resource for counsellors who wish to keep themselves up to date with advancements in the field of counselling. In addition, there is considerable growth in organisations that are offering welfare and support resources for their employees in conjunction with voluntary or charitable organisations offering online support resources for their clients. The book will illustrate how such services can be professionally serviced from an online perspective, in addition to a more traditional face-to-face service.

This book illustrates the practicalities of developing an online counselling and emotional support service, whilst also encompassing areas where online counselling skills can assist allied professionals to develop a service which has greater flexibility and accessibility for their service users. The field of student and peer mentoring can be particularly enhanced by computer-mediated communication (Sampson et al., 1997).

Terminology used within the book

As this book is intended as a resource for professionals and trainees working and studying across a diverse range of helping and support activities, I have elected to use the term 'client' to identify the person(s) accessing a service provision and the term 'practitioner' to identify the professional who uses counselling skills in their online professional practice. This terminology provides generic terms which do not restrict the scope of trainees and practitioners across a diverse range of services in seeking an informative and detailed illustration of the skills required when working online with clients. Where simulated examples of client work are included in chapters to illustrate online skills in practice, I have endeavoured to include examples which are not biased towards a specific gender or other related personal differences or circumstances. Such examples are not based upon actual client material and any similarities that may occur are purely conjured.

The book is also intended as a practical guide for practitioners who are engaged in online interactions with service users, or trainees who are considering the potential to include online working as an adjunct to their face-to-face practice. Therefore, I have included references which will illustrate research in this field of work, whilst also reinforcing experience based upon my online clinical practice. Further resources, skill development activities, and other invaluable aids to assist professional practice are available through the companion website to this book.

The book is divided into two parts. Part I consists of five chapters which focus on providing the reader with a clear outline of the practical skills required to develop and maintain an online relationship. This includes both brief interactions or longer-term associations. The necessary skills for effective online communication are further highlighted with the use of simulated service user examples illustrating the skills in practice. The reader is also encouraged to undertake exercises on their own, or as a shared activity, in order to gain deeper insight into the skills in practice and explore further considerations relating to the chapter subject and their specific area of professional practice. Part I also discusses the process for trainees and practitioners to establish their suitability for working online with clients and highlights the importance of online counselling training, skills experience, and technology know-how.

Part II contains four chapters where guidance and thought to professional and ethical considerations promote further thinking around the necessary requirements for professional practice. The reader is encouraged, through the use of questions and suggested exercises, to assess/reflect upon how the subject of professional and ethical considerations can be developed within their own related client work, whilst also consolidating the direction of practical guidance and skill acquirement provided within Part I.

References

Murphy, L. and Mitchell, D. (1998) 'When writing helps to heal: e-mail as therapy', *British Journal of Guidance & Counselling*, 26 (1): 12–21.

Pergament, D. (1998) 'Internet psychotherapy: current status and future regulation', *Health Matrix: Journal of Law Medicine*, 8 (2): 233.

Sampson, J.P. Jr., Kolodinsky, R.W. and Greeno, B.P. (1997) 'Counseling on the information highway: future possibilities and the potential problems', *Journal of Counseling & Development*, 75 (3): 10.

Trepal, H. Haberstroh, S., Duffey, T. and Evans, M. (2007) 'Considerations and strategies for teaching online counseling skills: establishing a relationship in cyberspace', *Counselor Education & Supervision*, 46: 266.

Zelvin, E. (2003) 'Treating addictions in cyberspace', *Journal of Social Work Practice in the Addictions*, 3 (3): 105–112.

ACKNOWLEDGEMENTS

Gaining the knowledge, clinical experience, and time required to write this book would not have been possible without the support of professional colleagues, online clients and supervisees, and my dear husband, Paul.

I would like to extend my thanks to all who have contributed both directly and indirectly to the completion of this piece of work.

INTRODUCTION

Welcome to *Online Counselling and Guidance Skills: A Resource for Trainees and Practitioners*. I hope that you will find this book and the companion website a valuable resource in understanding and applying online counselling skills within your sphere of professional practice. The book is not intended to direct practitioners in the practical use of the numerous variations in computer-mediated communication (CMC) tools and resources which are available for engaging online with clients: the primary purpose is to provide guidelines on the underpinning skills. These are transferable across all such contexts of establishing an online presence and, as such, this book will serve as an ongoing resource and reference point regardless of new developments within online computer-mediated technology and available online communication tools.

Who the book is for

In order to point out the audience for whom this book will be a valuable reading resource, I consider it relevant to draw a distinction between the contexts of professional practice where counselling skills are utilised and are identified in two categories:

- *Group 1* Professionals who use counselling skills within an ethical and boundaried framework, whilst working therapeutically with clients, and are defined as counsellors/therapists working within psychological services.
- *Group 2* A second cluster of professionals who are employed within allied health and social care, mental health, and guidance fields who use counselling skills within their work to enhance their relationships and communication with clients. Within this second group, I would also include those based in an academic setting where the provision of online support and guidance to students is a feature of their work. An example of this would be a tutor providing online tutorial support, facilitating online discussion groups, and podcasts, or a professional who is interacting with and providing support to service users online.

Counselling skills as an everyday communication tool

Even though we may not take time to reflect upon how the use of counselling skills features within our everyday activities, it is important to acknowledge that such skills are an integral aspect of our daily communication and support of others. It may be that we are listening to a colleague who requests information and guidance, or a friend who needs someone to talk to about an issue which is impacting upon their emotional well-being. In a professional context of providing support to others, counselling skills are in use throughout interactions with service users. In such instances, we use basic counselling skills to aid our understanding and offer of support. It would therefore be appropriate to consider how our use of counselling skills can be effectively adapted to an online environment. This book will be a useful resource within all these contexts. It would therefore be appropriate for those who are working online in a counselling, support, or helping capacity to seek information and guidance which will develop and enhance online communication skills, whilst also recognising that the book can be a useful resource for those who are regularly interacting with others in an online context. This book will be a valuable resource in either context.

How the book can be employed by trainees and practitioners

Working and interacting online in a counselling and support capacity takes a different guise to face-to-face working and therefore appropriate training is necessary, in addition to the traditional route of counselling skills study, to provide a professional and ethical presence online. This book is targeted at readers who hold an interest in online communication. You may be either embarking on training in this area of counselling skills use, or are interested in informing yourself, trainees, or colleagues of the skills required when working therapeutically or in a helping capacity online. The book can be used as a guide in two ways:

- in the early stages of enquiry into understanding or learning online counselling skills; or
- revisited as a reference point when using online counselling skills within client work.

The book is written in a straightforward manner with references to historical evidence of using written therapeutic interventions in client work and the current development of typed text counselling practice being applied online.

The main body of the book focuses on the necessary practical skills for working online in a helping or counselling capacity. Examples provided demonstrate these skills being utilised in pieces of simulated client work. There are prompts for the reader to reflect on their understanding within each chapter and also encouragement to consider how they can then transfer this to their framework for working online. As a general rule, there are distinct differences within interacting online, predominantly, as usually both parties are required to communicate without auditory or visual cues. The practitioner and service user will be working to establish and maintain a relationship online and endeavour to express themselves effectively with an absence of certain communication aids which are normally at hand when interacting in a face-to-face setting. It is therefore important to consider how this can impact on the relationship and the manner in which a beneficial relationship and successful outcome are achieved.

There are currently many variations to the electronic mediums available for online interaction. The primary distinction of online communication is defined as interacting synchronously (in real time) or asynchronously (with a time-delayed response). When communicating in each context, there will be a requirement to consider slight adaptations to skills applied in order to achieve optimum results.

Within this book, the term 'online interaction' will encompass all counselling skills communication which occurs using computer-mediated technology, unless specifically differentiating on the method used to illustrate a difference which is pertinent to a point being made.

The purpose of the book

There is no doubt that we are experiencing an increasing global awareness of the benefits gained from appropriate use of computers and the Internet. This may be for either personal, training, or professional purposes. The online Microsoft Press Centre (Microsoft, 2006) found that communication methods changed considerably during the period of 1996–2006, highlighting that in 1996, 24 per cent of the UK population owned a computer, compared to 62 per cent in 2006. Figures state only 6 per cent of UK households held Internet access in 1996, compared to 58 per cent of UK households in 2006.

There are some who may still prefer the more 'traditional' medium for communicating, learning, and conducting business, such as letters and using the telephone. Nonetheless, interacting with others via an electronic medium is increasing, and no doubt will continue to do so as it becomes a central interactive communication tool. *eTForecasts 2007*, as cited by Internet Statistics Compendium (2008), state that there were 1,173,109,925 global Internet users in October 2007, with the UK being the highest users within Europe.

Microsoft (2006) identified a membership of 270 million Hotmail account users worldwide in 2006. The introduction of email as a communication tool is now commonplace. Lago (1996) stresses that email counselling is a one-step extension to the most frequently used medium of accessing counselling support, that being telephone counselling.

As growth in technology and computer usage continues to expand, traditional routes for accessing support will naturally be facilitated by engaging with clients through CMC. The movement is accelerating further by the demand from clients as the younger generation of today and tomorrow (who will already be familiar with, and favour, electronic communication) naturally progress into the age bracket of the counselling and support user group. At the time of writing, there is evidence to suggest that online interaction and communication is a resource which is more widely used by females than males (Mindlin, 2007). With the traditional leaning towards this being apparent within face-to-face support, mental health, and therapeutic services, there is a requirement for online service providers to consider how males can be encouraged to engage in computer-mediated support and identify current potential barriers.

The rapid development of online counselling and support services within diverse areas such as higher and further education, careers guidance, mental health services, and so on further supports the argument for providing such a resource. Research and project evaluations which have been conducted within this context of online practice have not been widely disseminated or publicised outside of this sector to assist in the promotion of such adjuncts to face-to-face provision. Wherever possible, I would encourage organisations to broaden the scope of publishing such information as this will assist in raising the profile and outcomes from online service delivery. The book's companion website includes hyperlinks to such available reports and articles.

Evidence to substantiate confidence in the potential for online therapy and support services proving beneficial to service users can be highlighted by SAMHSA (a division of the US Health and Human Services) awarding a grant of 6 million dollars to four US e-therapy projects in 2007 (see etherapy law.com/?cat=6).

This book is aimed at those professionals who are already working online with service users as well as those who are seeking information and guidance on how to apply online counselling skills. As already stated, there are differences which naturally occur in online working and the book illustrates this in a manner which encourages the reader to consider how effective practice is achieved, whilst also provoking thought on variations within theoretical orientation which individual practitioners may wish to reflect upon when considering how their online practice can be developed.

Current movements in delivering counselling and support services using the Internet

The Internet provides a platform for social networks and interactive meeting places for people of all generations, using a vast catalogue of resources such as myspace.com and facebook.com, and is proving to be a convenient tool for communicating positively with others in a global capacity. The advent of the Internet has revolutionised many people's personal lives, work, and commercial activities as it holds the capability to transform the nature of traditional written correspondence and verbal interaction which is required to conduct everyday aspects of our life. However, it is not detrimental to the quality of communication achieved. There is some scepticism that electronic communication does not hold the potential to convey verbal or written narrative in the same meaningful way as traditional communication, due to a belief that the personalised style and physical characteristics of an individual are not present or conveyed in the same manner. One significant area of online activity has been the emergence of providing therapeutic support to service users where once the traditional route of face-to-face support has been the most common preferred option.

It is my aim within the book to illustrate how individual personality and forms of expression, alongside clear relational features, combine together when working online to create a robust relationship with service users and clients where successful therapeutic or support outcomes can be achieved.

In a work and commercial context, email has become a preferred mechanism for informing and making requests of colleagues or associates, whilst also used extensively for personal interaction with friends, family, and so on. Utilising Internet technology can speed up the process of giving or receiving information. There is the added advantage of being able to access this facility from within our office or home and make contact across a global setting.

The purpose of this book is to assist practitioners across a global setting in considering the appropriateness of transferring into or adopting an online practice, whilst also offering guidance in effective use of counselling skills during communication with clients. I do hope that this book serves to address some of the scepticism which is evident amongst professionals who are reluctant to acknowledge the place of online support and therapeutic services. There is a wealth of available discussion on the subject in conjunction with research evidence indicating success in areas of online therapeutic interventions to a level over and above that which is achieved in the more traditional resources available to clients. Research evidence indicates that theoretical modalities such as cognitive behavioural therapy (CBT) are transferable to computer-mediated interaction for clients suffering with anxiety and depressive disorders. cCBT Ltd (2007) claim to achieve significant outcomes with their online products, equivalent to face-to-face therapy, whilst also increasing access to mental health support for clients who may not otherwise come forward due to reasons such as stigma. The overall success of the project is no doubt influenced by the comparative costs involved in health services maintaining equivalent face-to-face service provisions, in conjunction with the potential for cCBT to reduce waiting lists for CBT treatment.

Excitement versus scepticism

The movement towards developing and implementing an online service delivery will be governed by the relevance, benefits, and suitability to the particular client groups with whom professionals currently work and seek to serve. Where organisations are not offering the facility of synchronous or asynchronous resources, there is usually a website presence where information and assistance can be accessed or downloaded. The general public readily engages with such facilities, and one might assume there is a general preconception that information and support should be readily available by conducting an Internet search for available support and guidance resources. With such a potential welcoming and captive client base, it is appropriate for service providers to consider how they might develop online services to clients where there are obvious advantages in doing so. In retaining a closed mind to such opportunities, professionals may lose the potential to increase access in areas where their online presence could be beneficial to both clients and themselves. This is particularly so as there is a general acceptance of counselling and mental health facilities being traditionally more accessible to those who are advantaged in social and financial position, therefore increasing their potential above others to secure the emotional support they need. Online support is not a less equivalent service and can provide an alternative which is potentially within the financial resource availability for those who cannot afford to access a face-to-face service.

With the increase in support and guidance, providers embracing the opportunity to move into securing an online presence with clients find that online communication creates a potential networking opportunity to raise the profile of such activity, provide reassurances in effective practice, and form a voice to encourage professional bodies in considering how such services can be more appropriately regulated and sit alongside face-to-face services, without the hindrance of being viewed by some as a second best option for clients, or a 'stop gap' for face-to-face resources.

I express the importance of those professionals and services who offer an online resource to clients to ensure that they guide their service users towards validating the authenticity of both the online service and the professionals who practise within it. In this way, clients have the opportunity to confirm the validity of a service and gain reassurance that they are being supported by bona fide professionals, in conjunction with enhancing the profile of this feature of professional practice. There are many online directories where professionals or services can be listed following certified evidence of their credentials and then have this information available to potential clients.

Whilst acknowledging any apparent resistance or scepticism, the opportunity of communicating and interacting with others in an online perspective is becoming firmly established within the global psyche and requires consideration as to how this influences the way in which counselling skills can be transferred to an online setting. There are many groups of professionals who are transferring aspects of their practice to establish an Internet and computer-mediated presence, both for the benefit of their service users and for achieving a more accessible and flexible service. The book will serve as a valuable resource where this is the case.

Historical research evidence relating to Internet and narrative therapy

When reviewing the historical evidence of counselling and psychoanalytical practice and research, it became apparent how significant a part both verbal and written narrative has played in establishing counselling practice as we know it today. The face-to-face aspect of counselling hinges in the main on working with the client's verbal narrative, with written narrative being utilised as an adjunct to practice in areas of counselling theoretical modalities. There is strong research evidence which indicates that therapeutic practice using written narrative as its primary focus has achieved positive outcomes for client work (Pennebaker and Beall, 1986, cited by Baum, 1997).

Pergament (1998) discusses in detail how Freud, Kleine, and Winnicott can be defined as antecedents of Internet psychotherapy by introducing deviations to the settings and parameters of traditional therapy and subsequently were defined as 'masters and mavericks' within their field for adopting such creativity in their client work.

It could therefore be deemed as completely appropriate to move what has been a more traditional aspect of written narrative into the medium of online work and develop online counselling skills practice from this stance. Suler (2003) indicates that self-expression through an electronic medium such as an email is representative of a constructed aspect of self which is conveyed through a more visible, permanent, concrete, and objective format than that available in speech.

There have been numerous studies which have investigated the effectiveness of Internet-based counselling and support in a global context. Within specific areas of symptom presentation, it has proven to be affective. These include depressive disorders (Christensen et al., 2004; Robertson et al., 2006), anxiety disorders (Kenardy et al., 2003), and some somatic disorders (Strom et al., 2000).

In the research undertaken by Christensen et al., patients suffering with depression were offered online support for the condition backed up by professionals who monitored their progress. There was evidence of between 53 per cent to 84 per cent adherence to the programme, with severity ratings for the disorder reducing from mid to mild when patients reached their eighth session.

Available choices in computer-mediated technology for online interactions

There are numerous options available to online practitioners in available CMC tools. If choosing webcams or video-conferencing facilities, both the client and practitioner may feel a stronger sense of being face-to-face. The use of encrypted synchronous chat, Internet forums, or web-conferencing facilities gives the option of online meetings where distance is an obstacle for all parties to be synchronously engaged within one physical locality. Such meetings can be a useful supplement to email exchanges or telephone/Skype exchanges. Synchronous resources can also prove to be a complementary adjunct to forum groups. Developments in existing resources and tools for engaging online with clients will continue, but the core online counselling skills required for effective service delivery and establishing a presence and online relationship with clients will remain pertinent within any such processes of development and change.

About the author: Jane Evans MA BACP (Accredited Member)

The author has extensive experience of designing and delivering student training programmes, counselling, online counselling, counselling supervision, and counselling consultancy, spanning 23 years. Her professional roles as trainer, counsellor, supervisor, and consultant have been based within such settings as the voluntary sector, local government, private practice, university and college counselling, youth work, education, and counselling services. Since 2003, Jane has piloted and developed online counselling services within a university setting, whilst also establishing her private online counselling and online supervision practice and the provision of certificated Online Counselling and Guidance Skills, Online Supervision and other online counselling skills courses through her website: www.ocst.co.uk. There are currently a broad range of services available to members of the public, trainees, practitioners, lecturers, and organisations via the website. In addition, Jane has written articles for the AUCC journal which have provided illustrations of how online counselling can be developed and managed within a university and further education context. She has also written a pull-out guide which directs practitioners to the ethical, legal, and professional considerations when developing and delivering online counselling skills using computer-mediated technology. Writing *Online Counselling and Guidance Skills: A Resource for Trainees and Practitioners*, and the companion website content, is a culmination of her knowledge and experiences within the broad range of professional activities that Jane has been engaged in since 1985.

References

Baum, A. (1997) *Cambridge Handbook of Psychology: Health and Medicine.* Cambridge: Cambridge University Press. p. 105.

cCBT Ltd. (2007) Available at www.ccbt.co.uk.

Christensen, H., Griffiths, K.M. and Jorm, A.F. (2004) 'Delivering interventions for depression by using the internet: Randomized controlled trial', *British Medical Journal*, 328: 265–9.

Lago, C. (1996) 'Computer therapeutics', *Counselling Journal of British Association for Counselling*, 7 (4): 287–9.

Internet Statistics Compendium (2008) *eTForecasts 2007*. Available at www. e-consultancy.com.

Kenardy, J., McCafferty, K. and Rosa, V. (2003) 'Internet-delivered indicated prevention for anxiety disorders: a randomized controlled trial', *Behavioural and Cognitive Psychotherapy*, 31: 279–89.

Microsoft (2006) Microsoft Press Centre. Available at: www.microsoft.com/uk/press/content/presscentre/releases/2006/12/PR03764.mspx.

Mindlin, A. (2007) 'Girl power is in full force online', *New York Times*, 24 December. Available at www.nytimes.com/2007/12/24/technology/24drill.html?_r=3&ex=1356238800&en=7de90ae5b2083391&ei=5088&partner=rssnyt&emc=rss&oref=slogin&oref=slogin&oref=slogin.

Pergament, D. (1998) 'Internet psychology: current status and future regulation', *Health Matrix (Journal of Law Medicine)*, 98 (18): 233–79.

Robertson, L., Smith, M., Castle, D. and Tannenbaum, D. (2006) 'Using the Internet to enhance the treatment of depression', *Australasian Psychiatry*, 14 (4): 413–17. Available at http://pt.wkhealth.com/pt/re/ausp/abstract.00127911-200612000-0012.htm:jsessionid=GyJdYcbq9Nqy2QSK6pwy6BVbTMZvr6Dgs3L7JJfxzXSLJ7n9dxsJ!1267112738!181195629!8091!-1.

Strom, L., Pettersson, R. and Andersson, G. (2000) 'A controlled trial of self-help treatment of recurrent headache conducted via the Internet', *Journal of Consulting and Clinical Psychology*, 72: 113–20.

Suler, J. (2003) *E-mail Communication and Relationships*. Available at www.rider.edu/~suler/psycyber/index.html.

PART I

Practical Skills

One of the distinct features within the field of practice, where online counselling skills are adopted within client work, is a reliance on the practitioner feeling confident and capable with keyboard and computing skills. Competency in the use of technology and software which is adopted for computer-mediated communication (CMC) is also a necessity. System effectiveness and stability is an evident feature in this area of professional practice and requires knowledge and proficiency during the process of conducting the administration of day-to-day service delivery and instances where technology issues interfere with the potential to engage with clients.

Chapter 1 provides an opportunity for practitioners to review their existing skills and identify areas where development is required. Storage of client data and administration of systems which comply with ethical and legal requirements is an important feature within this field of practice, in conjunction with supporting clients in securing confidentiality and privacy of their communication with the practitioner. Guidance in all such areas is provided, with the inclusion of additional points of consideration to encourage thought in relation to individual requirements and variations which are apparent to both practitioners and organisations.

Chapters 2 to 5 illustrate the practical skills required for effective online engagement with clients, providing examples of skill deployment through the simulated case study examples provided.

In the context of online interactions, a practitioner is required to develop relationships in the absence of both the client's and their own physical presence, therefore being reliant on their ability to convey sufficient presence, which encourages a willingness for clients to connect and gain a positive experience from the online exchange. Employing the use of counselling skills holds many variations to those encountered in a face-to-face setting and as such requires appropriate expertise prior to embarking on providing a service delivery. Chapters 2 to 5 cover such skill development in detail whilst encouraging the reader to undertake exercises which promote confidence and competency in this field of professional practice.

Simulated client case study examples are provided throughout Part I to further illustrate the deployment of online counselling skills, whilst also illustrating the potential for practitioners to develop a personalised style of engaging with clients. Exercises, examples, and points for consideration are also key features of each chapter.

Further reading, references, resources, and skill development activities for each chapter can be sourced via the companion website to this book.

1 THE FOUNDATIONS: A FRAMEWORK FOR PRACTICE WHEN USING ONLINE COUNSELLING SKILLS

Online counselling skills presented in this chapter:

- Establishing practitioner suitability for adopting the use of counselling skills in an online context
- Confidence building when using counselling skills with computer-mediated technology
- Online counselling system stability and suitability – what to do in the event of technology breakdown
- The structure of effective practice and individual client sessions when using online counselling skills
- Online security procedures – encryption, third party access to messages
- Administration, management, and storage of client material

Exercises and vignettes are included within this chapter, demonstrating the skills in practice and encouraging thought on the subject matter discussed.

This chapter discusses features essential to the initial planning and forming of an online practice. Whether practitioners are feeling confident that they are ready to establish an online practice or are still wrestling with the ethos and practicalities of including this as a feature of their work, there are important considerations and necessary practical skills which are required prior to forming supportive and meaningful online exchanges with clients. The evident client demands for extended ways of communicating with practitioners necessitates all who are comfortable with computer-mediated technology, as well as sceptics who dismiss its relevance within therapeutic and other areas of support and guidance practice, to reflect on the potential personal and professional rationale for denying its relevance to inclusion within current service delivery

(Green and Oldham, 2006). There are particular challenges, specifically for those who work with the young generation of clients and who have embedded computer-mediated technology as an intrinsic feature of their consciousness, to adapt their professional practice to meet the needs of their clients (Meyer, 2006).

There are elements which form an underpinning framework for establishing professional online practice. There may be some practitioners who are 'chomping at the bit' to get started in their engagement with online clients; I would encourage you to take time to stand back and deliberate upon points within this chapter and undertake a self-assessment prior to implementing service delivery. Such a process specifically relates to determining personal aptitude and the potential for possessing sufficient levels of computer literacy, in conjunction with the ability to organise, manage, and undertake the administration of a client system utilising appropriate online communication tools. The assessment of practitioner competency prior to establishing an online practice is central to the process of forming an ethical practice (Anthony and Jamieson, 2005).

The online practitioner will require a reasonable level of competence in being able to resolve difficulties with online technology and equipment in circumstances which either hold the potential to, or actually cause, a break in communication with clients. This is particularly pertinent where a practitioner is working from home, or within an organisation where IT support resources are limited, and constrained by how they are able to assist practitioners in maintaining the required level of service to clients. In all instances where a practitioner is not comfortable with CMC and technology, it is recommended that they do not proceed to become established in online practice (Kraus et al., 2004).

Supporting clients within an online environment requires a different approach to that which is adopted in a face-to-face context, with confidence in a variety of both synchronous and asynchronous mediums. The experiencing of the 'other' can be more apparent within synchronous interactions than those encountered in asynchronous exchanges (Suler, 2000). Such dynamics will influence a practitioner's preference in the selected media for interacting with online clients.

The online practitioner will be structuring their practice to fit a framework which is consistent and user-friendly for clients, whilst also compliant with both professional and legal requirements. This chapter provides the opportunity to consider how such aspects can be adopted, developed, and applied to online practice and applicable to the practitioner's area of work or specialism.

This first chapter also provides an opportunity for trainees and practitioners to explore practical aspects of moving their professional practice into this field of working, and assess their present working pattern against aspects which will be required if intending to adopt the use of online counselling skills with clients.

Establishing practitioner suitability for adopting the use of counselling skills in an online context

Diversity in the range of circumstances where practitioners will be electing to utilise online counselling skills within their professional practice will bring variations regarding the allocation of time spent in engaging with clients. Using online counselling skills may feature as a minor element of professional practice or the primary source of connecting with clients. This is an important consideration, as the process of moving professional practice into this field requires the practitioner to conduct their association with clients without actual physical contact and potentially to work in isolation when not based in an environment with other colleagues in the close vicinity. It is therefore important for the practitioner to be comfortable working alone in conjunction with additional variations which are a feature in this area of specialism.

The checklist provided in Exercise 1.1 can assist in formulating an initial decision on practitioner potential for the required flexibility and enthusiasm to work online with clients given variations to time spent interacting with clients and the distinctive features in this sphere of professional practice.

EXERCISE 1.1

DETERMINING SUITABILITY

Use this checklist to help determine your suitability for adopting your counselling skills to an online setting.

1. Would I relate well to lone working using a computer as the vehicle for interacting with clients?
2. What proportion of my work would I be comfortable in transferring to an online setting?
3. Do I currently enjoy and feel comfortable when interacting with others through an online medium?
4. Am I content in working without the actual physical presence of clients?
5. Could I manage the administration and practicalities of an online office with the associated responsibilities and appointment system requirements?

Having explored the questions within Exercise 1.1, this may prompt further thought by readers in forming a decision in both the positive and negative impacts upon their professional practice if proceeding into this area of work. Within the context of professional online practice, it is relevant to plan a schedule with regular breaks away from the computer in between client work, during the process of administration, and management tasks of online practice. Consistently working for excessive periods using a computer is not advantageous to the professional or the resulting client work.

Other practical considerations apply in a similar manner to those professionals who spend considerable time sitting during their working day:

- Working online requires adherence to the appropriate setting up of a work station which is conducive to health, posture, and so on.
- It is important to maintain a good level of social interaction with others if employed in online work for long periods of the day, due to the absence of physical contact with others when engaged in this sphere of professional practice.
- Regular breaks away from the computer, in conjunction with exercise, to compensate for the sedentary nature of being based at a computer work station, are also beneficial.

Confidence building when using counselling skills with computer-mediated technology

Confidence and competency when interacting using asynchronous and synchronous online communication

Confidence and competency in the sphere of using counselling skills in an online context is represented by a practitioner having acquired a familiarity with interacting using computer-mediated communication (CMC), in conjunction with a self-assurance in the ability to manage meaningful and coherent exchanges using the variations in both synchronous and asynchronous communication tools which are adopted within their practice. Due to diversity and individual circumstances within services intending to or who actually utilise online counselling skills, this influences the potential and practicalities of service delivery. Prior to introduction, both the organisation and the practitioner should consider what mediums will be most suited to their service, in conjunction with forming a decision on the confidence and skills level which the practitioner possesses to deliver the facility within the scope of an ethical and professional framework. The ultimate goal of effective service delivery will be based upon two elements:

- Practitioners must be sufficiently confident and competent with the selected interaction tools and be aware of potential areas where security issues could lead to breaches of confidentiality, whilst also being proficient to a level where they have the ability to focus all of their attention on clients.

Where a practitioner experiences anxiety in using a selected medium, this will undoubtedly impact on the quality of the online exchanges.

- Selected computer-mediated applications and software must be compatible with the intended service delivery whilst also meeting identified security requirements. Speed and Ellis (2003) indicate that the majority of security breaches occur internally due to organisation structures and therefore identify authorisation and authentication as two key features in ensuring client confidentiality, whilst carefully selected firewalls assist in the prevention of external security risks. Connolly (2001) highlights a remote likelihood of external attack on individuals or small organisations as being insignificant due to the credibility and prestige to an individual for breaking through the security systems of such low-profile service providers serving no purpose.

In the process of an individual or organisation selecting the most appropriate online systems and resources which are compatible to competencies of the staff deployed to deliver the provision, the following points can be utilised in the decision-making process. These suggestions are not absolute as variations will be apparent and influenced according to individual circumstances:

1. What systems support is available to develop and maintain selected mediums utilised for engaging with clients?
2. Which mediums will be user friendly and compatible with client needs whilst also meeting security, ethical and professional requirements alongside practitioner and organisation requirements?
3. Are staff to be employed in the use of chosen medium(s) sufficiently confident and competent to provide the level of service and security required?
4. Where financial costs are involved, can the funds be guaranteed to develop and maintain consistency in the selected service delivery tools?

EXERCISE 1.2

SELECTING THE COMMUNICATION MEDIUM

How would each reader know they have acquired the necessary level of confidence and skill which is required to deliver an online practice using specific communication and interaction tools?

(Continued)

(Continued)

As a process of determining current skill levels and practical ability for use in an online perspective using various online communication tools, you might find it helpful to use the evaluation sheet in Figure 1.1. Alternatively, share this activity with someone who is familiar with your existing online communication as a process of gaining an enhanced sense of how others experience your current expertise in this area of interaction.

This exercise can also be used as a skill expansion checklist by trying out new tools with a colleague using asynchronous and synchronous communication, feeding back to each other on the suitability and effectiveness of each variation, in conjunction with assessing how effectively each person has conveyed themselves or managed within a new area of online interaction.

The evaluation sheet can be a valuable tool for trainers or supervisors of online counselling skills practice to assist in the professional development of their trainees and supervisees. It allows a scoring assessment, and space to enter development activities required to enhance the skill, and could also be developed to include space for detailed feedback when sharing the exercise with a colleague or when engaged in a professional development activity such as within a training or supervision setting.

For guidelines to available online communication software, details can be sourced from Wikipedia at en.wikipedia.org/wiki/ Social_software(2007).

Having identified your strengths and development areas using Figure 1.1, there is an opportunity to consider which feels the most comfortable and suitable media for you to develop as primary sources of online interaction tools. It is important to note at this point that any adopted resources should comply with requirements for confidentiality constraints within professional online practice.

By completing this exercise, it will provide the potential for you to gain insight into how clients who are not familiar with online communication tools might feel disinclined to engage with the service. Such insight can therefore assist with the process of developing resources which you intend to make available to clients with the aim of supporting their familiarity and confidence in using the chosen medium.

Question: Are you able to convey clear and effective communication using both synchronous and asynchronous online software tools which may include some or all of the following?		
Online communication method	**Skill level and feedback (Score 1–10)**	**Development activity required**

Email
Internet Relay Chat (IRC)
Online voice call,
  e.g. Skype
Online forum or web
  board discussion
Synchronous online
  group work
Video conferencing		

Figure 1.1 *Evaluation sheet for determining skill levels and practical ability in online communication*

Online counselling system stability and suitability – what to do in the event of technology breakdown

Confidence and competency in managing disruptions caused by technology issues

To ensure an effective service to clients, the practitioner should be confident in communicating electronically to a point where unaccounted for interruptions, due to technology issues or temporary breakdown in connection, do not create a level of anxiety which is evident or transparent to clients. Where a lack of confidence or skill with the medium and an inability to rectify minor technology issues are apparent, this will prevent full concentration being applied to the online interaction and could lead to an unsatisfactory outcome and possible loss of confidence in the practitioner's potential to 'contain' an online session in a professional manner which is free from external interference. Where using online counselling skills is a new feature for a practitioner, or when in the process of adopting a new communication tool for interacting with clients, there will be a period of time where full competency and confidence is developed prior to achieving 'unconscious competence' with either the synchronous or asynchronous selected medium(s).

During this period, it is important that the practitioner seeks to gain the required skill level through activities which do not involve clients. One of the difficulties which may be encountered when developing new skills in this field of work is the practitioner requiring another person or persons to interact with to develop their online skills. This is where the feature of training, which is provided within an online learning environment, is invaluable. Colleagues can also be a beneficial resource for experimenting with and developing new online skills or for trying out new sources of computer-mediated technology and software.

Online forums, discussion groups, or online counselling support organisations are useful vehicles for developing skills and knowledge, whilst also promoting a deeper understanding of the experience of being supported by others in an online context and therefore increases empathic understanding in how clients will experience using an online service.

🄴🅇🄴🅁🄲🄸🅂🄴   🄳.🄳

SUPPORT AND TRAINING REQUIREMENTS

When reflecting upon your current skills and knowledge of technology issues which may impact upon service delivery, consider what support and training you may require to minimise the potential for disruption to client service delivery.

The structure of effective practice and individual client sessions when using online counselling skills

The structure of effective practice

There are many variations in how organisations offering online services are structured. Within all such variations, there are underpinning features which require consideration during the process of defining how an online client resource will be structured and delivered. This section provides details regarding such considerations.

There are several underpinning requirements for effective structuring of an online practice using counselling skills:

1. Where a service is provided via a website or online portal, this should be accessible, reliable and consistent, user friendly, and promote a positive experience for clients and generate a sense of trust in the efficacy of the service (Briggs et al., 2002). These points also apply to the selected medium and software which is adopted for interacting with clients.

2. Selected online mediums and software should have an encryption and password facility, particularly where online therapeutic work or a supervision facility is provided, and prevent both internal and external unauthorised intrusion (Speed and Ellis, 2003). In addition, all adopted resources should be reviewed and updated in adherence to ethical practice (BACP, 2005).

3. If clients are required to make a payment for accessing the service, there should be a range of methods available which are secure and straightforward to use.

4. Where appointment systems are a feature of the service, both the organisational structure and the online practitioners' management of these arrangements should be consistent and effective in meeting client needs. Where cancellations or rearrangement of allocated appointments occur, this should be communicated to clients via an agreed channel, which may include an alternative to online contact, particularly where a technology issue is apparent.

5. Online netiquette and contract boundaries should be agreed with service users, which will vary to some degree, dependent on the nature of the service provided.

6. In the field of online support and counselling practice, clients should be provided with alternative sources of assistance if the organisation or practitioner is not accessible by a 24-hour, 7-day per week service provision.

7. Where client data is stored by either the practitioner or institution, the systems employed for doing so should be clearly conveyed to service users. Adopted systems must comply with legal, ethical and professional guidelines.

An example which highlights these initial elements of structure within a therapeutic context is provided in Box 1.1. This simulated client example will feature as a continuation in each chapter as an example to assist readers through the skill and knowledge development stages in this book, and is distinguished from other examples by the use of * in conjunction with its Box number.

Box 1.1* Simulated client example – Sam

Julie has recently commenced working online with clients in independent practice. She has received an email enquiry regarding online counselling through her website email account. Julie's website provides clear, user-friendly information and guidance for potential clients including the nature of

(Continued)

(Continued)

online counselling, the computer-mediated approaches included within service delivery, the process for requesting appointments, and so on. The potential client, Sam, has only provided brief details of personal issues and has not given any medical history. Julie replies to Sam requesting further information, whilst also providing a brief illustration of the facilities she provides and attaches a client assessment/agreement which she requests Sam to read through and return, raising any resulting queries in the content as required.

The document outlines:

- What a client can expect from the online counsellor and boundaries of the online relationship.
- Information relating to maintaining Internet privacy and security of asynchronous communication.
- Further details relating to Julie's qualifications and experience, with details of how this can be verified.
- A request for telephone contact details in the event of technology breakdown and GP details, together with a full explanation of the purpose in requesting such details.
- A request for information relating to current or past relevant medical or mental health issues, with guidance notes.
- Arrangements for appointments and response time to contact from clients, including arrangements for missed appointments.
- Details regarding the management, dissemination, and storage of any personal and therapeutic records during and following completion of the contract for counselling, including a brief explanation of how client information is utilised for the purpose of clinical supervision.

A list of additional features which can be included within such client agreements can be sourced from an example client contract given in the companion website to this book.

In this first reply, Julie also directs the client to specific pages on her website where relevant information relating to her service delivery can be located. She encourages Sam to engage in a brief sequence of email exchanges during the process of assessing the suitability for online counselling in meeting Sam's individual needs and circumstances. Julie is also aware that some clients make an initial approach to online services without continuing through to arrange an appointment. With this in mind, she includes details of emergency services that provide online support in the event of the client choosing not to reply to her email.

E X E R C I S E   1 .4

STRUCTURE OF EFFECTIVE PRACTICE

The underpinning foundation requirements for an effective framework when applying online counselling skills were presented and discussed above. Consider what additional factors you will need to take into account that are specific to the context of service delivery where you intend to, or currently, adopt the use of online counselling skills.

How might your own approach to the initial stages of contact with clients differ from those identified in the example provided in Box 1.1?

How might the illustrated approach and content of client agreement/assessment contrast to your preferred personal and professional style for communicating within your online service structure and your intended components of service delivery?

The structure of individual client sessions or meetings when using online counselling skills

This section builds upon the initial illustration relating to a framework for establishing an online practice by presenting a structure for individual meetings with clients.

If you are already using face-to-face counselling skills in a therapeutic context, or have given formal presentations to others, you will be familiar with the format used in ensuring the required delivery structure – this being that each 'session' or presentation has a beginning, middle, and end phase. When using counselling skills online in the setting of a formal meeting with a client, the same framework applies, with some additional elements which form the complete composition of an online session. There are further variations, dependent on whether asynchronous or synchronous communication is being employed.

The framework of sessions or meeting times which individual practitioners will adopt in their online practice will vary according to professional contexts. It is important to identify and clarify the parameters of time available at the onset of client interactions. Rosenfield (1997) emphasises this point when referring to telephone counselling interactions, and the same level of significance applies during online interactions. The structure of cognitive behavioural therapy (CBT) sessions will require a more structured approach than the format identified below, and would usually include homework

(Sanders, 1996). Vocational guidance counselling includes the use of specific objectives within each session (Seema, 2005).

The structure of an asynchronous session (occurring with a time-delayed response)

- *Beginning phase*   Open with a greeting. This is best offered in a reciprocal form to that adopted by the client, such as Hello, Hi, and so on.

    If there are particular aspects of your reply which you would want a client to be alert to, such as a concern which has arisen from reading their last communication or a primary point(s) you wish to convey, then this can be included in the beginning with a clear explanation of why it has been highlighted in this way. Some practitioners may prefer to include this at the end of the written narrative, but this increases the chance of it being over-looked by the client. A general empathic statement may also be placed within the opening section of the communication as an indication to a client that any particular features conveyed by a client in their previous response have been heard and responded to by the practitioner. In circumstances where there has been no previous communication with a client, empathic reassurance from the practitioner to the client is beneficial.

    Avoid including too much detail in the beginning phase as it is likely that a client has been eagerly awaiting a reply and may be put off by a lengthy introduction to the main content.

    It is preferable to distinguish clearly the opening subject matter within a defined paragraph, before going on to the middle content of the communication.
- *Middle phase*   This section contains the 'body' of dialogue which the practitioner is intending to convey to a client and will include some or all of the following, dependent on the context of the service provision where the practitioner is employed: questions, empathic responses, paraphrasing, information, feedback, guidance, summarising and reflection upon material from the client's previous communication; suggestions on how the client can progress with moving forward in their presenting issues; seeking clarification on aspects of content from previous communication; providing clarification to a client where a misunderstanding or an aspect of confusion over previous content has occurred.
- *End phase*   This phase will contain variations which are influenced by the context of the practitioner's professional practice, but in the main the final section of synchronous communication provides an opportunity for the practitioner to reinforce any specific features of the main body content that they wish the client to hear, whilst also closing the communication with an expression of positive intent towards the client. Often within an ongoing therapeutic or supportive context, a practitioner will include a 'sign off' where they offer an expression of looking forward to receiving subsequent contact from the client, whilst also wishing the client well.

The structure of a synchronous session **(occurring in real time using a text-formed exchange)** A clear distinction in synchronous communication is the fact that practitioner and client meet in real time and as such this requires further attention to effective time management to allow for appropriate structuring of the interaction. Due to both parties being engaged in a variety of practical tasks including typing, looking at the computer screen, constructing thoughts, and responding to the other person, the content of an exchange is reduced in comparison to that which is experienced in a face-to-face meeting. There may be instances where practitioners are supplementing synchronous client work with asynchronous communication; this may require variations in the content of the beginning phase to account for the linking of discussion threads which have been formed in either instance.

- *Beginning phase* The practitioner opens the meeting with a greeting and welcomes the client. When engaged in a continuing online relationship, the practitioner may ask if there are any issues that have arisen since the last contact with the client that they wish to be included within the current meeting. If the practitioner is employed in a counselling or supportive role, they will then invite the client to identify a focus for the session, or assist the client in identifying a focus. In professional circumstances, where the practitioner is guiding the online exchange, they would usually take the lead at this point.
- *Middle phase* As defined in the asynchronous example, this section will contain the elements of questions, empathic responses, paraphrasing, information, feedback, guidance, summarising and reflection upon material from the client's previous communication, suggestions, seeking clarification on aspects of content from previous communication, or providing clarification. In a therapeutic or supervision context, this section may also include some creative or 'playful' exploration of relevant material presented by the client. In a setting where the practitioner is predominantly the facilitator of the interaction, for example during a tutorial or presentation format, this section will be directed accordingly by the practitioner.
- *End phase* The ending of a synchronous meeting should be carefully timed and managed in order to accommodate an appropriate conclusion to relevant subject matter which has been identified as the focus for the interaction whilst also providing the client with a sense of containment in the context of therapeutic exchanges. Where time-allotted appointment systems are used with clients, the process of managing an effective ending to synchronous interactions will have increased significance as it would be unprofessional to run over into another client's appointment time. Waiting for a practitioner to make contact for a scheduled appointment in an online setting can be distressing for clients and should not feature within professional practice.

Additional considerations   When applying online counselling skills during a first meeting with a client in either a synchronous or asynchronous context, there will be additional considerations to those identified, especially assisting the client to feel relaxed and familiar with the service and the practitioner who is to be providing the online interaction. This is a particularly important feature within an online perspective due to the absence of actual physical presence. Both parties are solely reliant on forming a positive relationship and therapeutic working alliance through the selected online medium without the benefits and nuances which are apparent in face-to-face exchanges (Ainsworth, 2001).

Online security procedures – encryption, third party access to messages

In instances where all communication is directed through an organisation's website or online portal, there is an increased potential to manage control over how clients access and receive their interaction with a practitioner, particularly in circumstances where clients access the service through a secure gateway. The physical location where a client accesses the service is reliant on the client's choice. There is a responsibility for informing clients of security and privacy issues and providing guidelines on how to ensure the privacy of both synchronous and asynchronous exchanges. It cannot be assumed that these have been followed by clients and that they are taking appropriate steps to ensure confidentiality or to prevent a third party being able to view content by leaving their computer unattended or unprotected. It is therefore advisable to place any personal or confidential material in an attachment if communication is being conducted through a process of non-website managed email exchanges, and if possible use password protection for the opening of attachments. In the case of synchronous interaction and asynchronous exchanges, it is necessary to adopt an encryption facility whilst re-iterating guidelines where relevant regarding the maintenance of privacy and security.

Administration, management, and storage of client material

The systems used for storage of client material will vary according to the resources available to the practitioner. This will also be influenced by such circumstances as working independently with clients or being employed by an organisation which has specific systems in place for holding client data. There are legal requirements for individuals and institutions that hold and store personal data from client sources, including those who handle or store personal information relating to clients accessing a service. Such storage is governed by the Data Protection Act 1988. Legal and security issues are central to decision making (Connolly, 2001). For those professionals conducting their work within the UK, information is available from www.ico.gov.uk (Information Commissioner's Office, 2008).

In basic terms, the 1988 Act directs any person or organisation to follow certain guidelines to ensure that personal information is:

- fairly and lawfully processed
- processed for limited purposes
- adequate, relevant, and not excessive
- accurate and up to date
- not kept for longer than is necessary
- processed in line with the individual's rights
- secure
- not transferred to other countries without adequate protection.

Members of the public have a right to request details of any personal data held by an individual professional or organisation. It is therefore essential to plan for administration, management, and storage of client data in accordance with legal and ethical requirements that relate to the sphere of practice and the country where the practice is based. If your online practice is sourced from within an organisation, it is recommended that you seek advice and support from your legal services department if unclear regarding the implications for the specific requirements regarding the Act within your field of work.

For UK practitioners, it is advisable to check whether you require Data Controller status in the context of your online practice.

Summary

Moving into a field where the use of online counselling skills features in professional practice requires assessment and planning by both the practitioner and, where relevant, the organisations who support professionals to conduct an online practice. In all instances, both the professional and the organisation require the skills, resources, and administration skills to provide an ethical, legal, and consistent facility for clients. The distinct considerations which are apparent when transferring and using counselling skills in an online context, and the practicalities of applying their use, in conjunction with the broader context of structuring such a service as a whole, require careful planning and development in the process of adhering to both professional and legal requirements. There may be an assumption that transferring the use of counselling skills to an online context does not require specialist skills and competency. This is not the case (Anthony and Jamieson, 2005).

Points for consideration

- Having reflected upon the personal or organisational requirements which are necessary to progress with planning for using online counselling skills in client work, what training and additional resources will be required prior to proceeding implementation?
- What support do you need from within the organisation where you are employed in order to move forward with planning and developing an online practice?
- What research might you be able to undertake which would be advantageous in ascertaining the potential for existing service users to engage with an online practice, or transfer from the current face-to-face service provision?

References

Ainsworth, M. (2001) *Internet Therapy Guide: Types of Online Counselling Services.* Available at www.metanoia.org/imhs/type.htm.

BACP/Anthony, K. and Jamieson, A. (2005) *Guidelines for Online Counselling and Psychotherapy*, 2nd edition. Lutterworth: British Association for Counselling and Psychotherapy.

Briggs, P., Burford, B., De Angeli, A. and Lynch, P. (2002) 'The elements of computer credibility', *Social Science Computer Review*, 20 (3): 321–32.

Connolly, K.J. (2001) *Law of Internet Security and Privacy.* Aspen Publishers Online. Available at www.aspenpublishers.com.

Green, M.T. and Oldham, M. (2006) 'New technologies: new challenges', *AUCC Journal*. Winter edition. Available at www.aucc.uk.com/journal_pdf/winter 06_3.pdf.

Information Commissioner's Office (2008) *The Data Protection Act: Your Rights, Responsibilities to Data Protection.* Available at www.ico.gov.uk/what_we_cover/ data_protection.aspx.

Kraus, R., Zack, J. and Stricker, G. (2004) *Online Counselling: A Handbook for Mental Health Professionals.* San Diego, CA: Elsevier/Academic Press. p. 78.

Meyer, D. (2006) 'Student support – new directions. Internet: for good or ill', *AUCC Journal*. Winter edition. Available at www.aucc.uk.com/journal_pdf/winter06_7.pdf.

Rosenfield, M. (1997) *Counselling by Telephone.* London: Sage.

Sanders, D. (1996) *Counselling for Psychosomatic Problems.* London: Sage. p. 77.

Seema, Y. (2005) *Guidance and Counselling.* New Delhi: Anmol Publications. p. 235.

Speed, T. and Ellis, J. (2003) *Internet Security: A Jump Start for System Administrators and IT Managers.* St Louis: Digital Press/Elsevier.

Suler, J. (2000) *Psychology of Cyberspace: Hypotheses about Online Text Relationships.* Available at www-usr.rider.edu/~suler/psycyber/textrel.html.
Wikipedia (2007) *Social Software.* Available at en.wikipedia.org/wiki/Social_software.

Further reading, references, resources, and skill development activities relating to the subject matter within this chapter can be sourced via the companion website to this book.

2 ESTABLISHING AN ONLINE PRESENCE AND ONLINE RELATIONSHIP

Online counselling skills presented in this chapter:

- Defining the term 'online presence'
- Working without visual or auditory cues to establish an online presence and relationship
- The use of avatars to establish an online presence and develop an online relationship
- Establishing an online relationship
- The initial online interaction
- Forming a physical perspective of an online client
- Helping clients to help themselves – problem solving

Exercises and vignettes are included within this chapter, demonstrating the skills in practice and encouraging thought on the subject matter discussed.

This chapter will assist practitioners in building their understanding of utilising presence to enhance online interactions and relationships. Establishing an online presence and developing the skills required for engaging with a client during the initial stage of the online relationship, presenting a positive and supportive online presence, and maintaining this within a single or continued online relationship are key to the success of online client interactions. The practitioner's personal and relational skills are core attributes which are required for establishing effectiveness, whether engaged in face-to-face or online relationships.

Research evidence suggests there is a possibility for 'detachment' to be experienced by some clients when engaging with computer-mediated technology. This may indicate a potential for some individuals to develop anti-social behaviour patterns where a fantasy existence can become familiar, and potentially preferable, to the valuing of face-to-face relationships (Cooper, 2002).

Hamburger (2005) identifies frequent Internet service users as closely allied to introvert personality types.

It is pertinent to balance the advantages for individuals in seeking to establish an online presence and securing relevant, effective support in this manner against an apparent anxiety that online interactions could lead to individuals withdrawing from face-to-face contact and relationships. Research evidence does indicate that online therapy can create a working alliance which reciprocates qualities of relatedness encountered in face-to-face therapy and therefore highlights that a positive and effective online presence and therapeutic alliance can be achieved (Prado and Meyer, 2004).

Defining the term 'online presence'

As an illustration of what I am conveying by using the term 'online presence', I would ask you to reflect upon a personal relationship that you share with someone who is close to you on an emotional level. In addition to the personal qualities and characteristics that person possesses, I would ask you to reflect further based upon the question: beyond the personal qualities and individual characteristics of that person, what aspects of the person are you holding in your mind that establishes their unique characteristic of 'presence'? I think you may find that it is impossible to define this in a concise way. A person's presence is a representation of their self as a whole person, with a uniqueness where, even if all aspects of their being were transferred to another person, the actual essence of this person could not be represented within another human being. We could then assume that an individual's presence is similar to that of an individual's fingerprint and cannot be replicated. This being accepted, we could confirm that a person's presence is unique and defined by them alone.

In the context of online relationships and communication, such a presence is evident and can be experienced in a similar manner to that of face-to-face encounters as unique and not replicated in other clients. Such a process is experienced through sensory stimulation involving five key features:

- sensory stimulation from the environment
- change in the environment
- interactivity with the environment
- the degree of familiarity
- balance.
  (Suler, 2003)

The feature of establishing an online presence within helping interactions is a key element to acquiring empathy in respect of the client and material presented within online interactions, whilst also being an integral element of developing an online relationship. In face-to-face counselling interactions, presence is defined as non-verbal and is not conveyed through explicit gestures (Whitmore, 2004).

EXERCISE 2.1

ONLINE PRESENCE

Consider how you experience the 'presence' of someone who is familiar to you. How might aspects of their unique presence be conveyed using computer-mediated communication (CMC)?

Establishing an online presence

A core ethos of the person-centred model of psychotherapy and the practitioner who works within this framework is defined as a way of *being* as opposed to a method of *doing*, with this way of *being* coming naturally from the practitioner, whilst also providing a releasing and helpful experience for a client. Rogers (1980) defined the effect of presence in the context of therapeutic relationships as a meeting of inner spirits in which intense growth, healing, and energy are in attendance. I would like to begin by setting this ethos as a seed for growth in the term 'presence' as defined within this chapter, and in turn 'online presence', which is key to an online relationship.

When considering how this applies in online therapeutic and supportive relationships, it is important to consider the following. Supporting clients in an online context is directly comparative to face-to-face working when seeking to establish a presence. It defines the essence of both practitioner and client and initiates the development of empathy and understanding which in turn facilitates the process of relating successfully and the achievement of a positive pathway for the interaction and online relationship.

Each practitioner in either an online or face-to-face context will have unique personal and professional qualities and characteristics which contribute to them being distinctive to clients in conjunction with distinguishing features relating to their area of specialised practice. The personality and mannerisms displayed by the practitioner will be evident to clients and are key to the dynamics which assist in forming an alliance with those who seek support in both a face-to-face and an online perspective. Both practitioner and client establish a presence, with the practitioner's input being strategic to promoting a positive outcome.

Variations in service provision which can influence the characteristics and potential for developing an online presence

The potential for establishing and maintaining an online relationship can be influenced by the length of time and context in which you are working online with a client, and also the duration of the ongoing relationship. Such variations in contexts will usually fall into two groups:

- A service which offers a one-off interaction or the opportunity of ad hoc support where the client may not have access to the same practitioner on each occasion of accessing the service. In this context, the practitioner and client may have only one asynchronous exchange, or if working through a synchronous medium, the meeting will take place for one hour or less.
- A service which offers ongoing support where a client will have the opportunity to work with a designated practitioner during the period of seeking support. In this context, the practitioner and client will have synchronous or asynchronous exchanges over a sequence of contracted meetings.

In either of these variations, there will be the need for the practitioner to convey an online presence which assists the client in achieving a positive and beneficial experience, whilst also encouraging the user of the service to establish their own online presence, as would be the practice within a face-to-face supportive interaction.

Factors which can influence the potential for developing an effective online presence and relationship with service users

A client may present to a service with familiarity of working with a synchronous or asynchronous electronic medium, or they may have elected to seek support without having the confidence to communicate in this context. They may also feel apprehensive regarding online interaction and the sharing of personal information online. It is important during the initial stages of contact that the facilitator of the interaction assesses whether the client is adequately familiar with keyboard skills and possesses the potential to adapt to communicating through an electronic medium. It may be that the client presents in a brief and restricted way to a service, possibly due to experiencing anxiety regarding revealing personal information rather than having a weakness in written communication or possessing the appropriate online communication skills. Where the practitioner may conclude that this medium is not suitable for a client or their presenting issues, they should offer assistance in securing an appropriate referral, whilst explaining to the client the reasons for recommending this action.

Working without visual or auditory cues to establish an online presence and relationship

Visual and auditory conjectures will be absent when working online, unless the client has provided a visual picture of themselves, or the session is facilitated with a webcam or auditory facility. There are many other unique personal indications that may become apparent as the online interaction progresses. One of the necessary acquisitions for an online practitioner is developing an awareness of such inferences and utilising them to gain a deeper understanding and sense of clients and draw upon this information to establish and develop positive relationships. Making use of this skill will assist in the considerations a practitioner relies upon when forming responses to each client in a manner which enhances the practitioner's online presence.

There is research evidence to suggest that interaction in a face-to-face setting can prove to be a barrier in bringing issues relating to shame and other related emotions (Suler, 1997). If an online practitioner is providing the necessary supportive environment where a client is less restricted by these emotions, it can provide an enhanced opportunity for clients to engage as they are not physically present with a practitioner, which can release feelings of inhibition and reluctance. Working in a medium that is text-based, and has an absence of visual and auditory cues, can prove to be favourable/beneficial to clients as they may feel more relaxed and able to form a relationship in less time than might be taken in face-to-face working. This can occur when a client has the experience of being able to absorb themselves in a flow of words and dialogue during an exchange of thoughts and reflections with an online practitioner.

Suler (2003) indicates that transference responses can be prominent in online communication, and greatly enhanced versus face-to-face interactions due to the absence of a physical perspective of the person. Transference dynamics can be a key factor to the potential outcome of a therapeutic relationship and require consideration by the online practitioner in understanding how this might be impacting in a negative or positive manner on the development and maintenance of the online relationship.

⸻

EXERCISE 2.2

NON-VISUAL COMMUNICATION

Consider how your style of communication presentation differs within face-to-face interactions and those conducted through CMC such as email.

Which of the two interaction formats would provide a more comfortable platform for you to discuss uncomfortable or difficult feelings about yourself?

What could a conveyer of online communication offer you which would increase your willingness to disclose feelings or thoughts that are uncomfortable

⸻

The use of avatars to establish an online presence and develop an online relationship

Avatars provide a fascinating subject for discussion and play an important role in online interpersonal dynamics and the potential for projection and transference. Adopted online personas or identity can be evident in many forms, even within email account identity. Consider your initial response to receiving two separate email enquiries from potential clients, one of which is 'darknightofdeath@hotmail.com' in contrast with 'tinkerbell@yahoo.co.uk'. Such personal 'labelling' immediately conjures a picture and persona of the email account holder, and may have been selected without considering the deeper symbolic meanings (Suler, 2003).

Nowak and Rauh (2005) discuss how online personas and relationships can be enhanced by the use of anthropomorphic characteristics such as avatars by providing a more engaging, likeable, and credible online image, as this fits the human need to have a visual identification of someone or something we are interacting or forming a relationship with. Avatars can be useful in gaining a sense of another person when visual characteristics are absent, as they can be selected by individuals and hold either conscious or unconscious representations of these individuals. They can be used to portray aspects or attributes which a person identifies with, or which they hope to possess. Avatars can be used to heighten or blanket aspects of race and culture (Nakamura, 2002). Avatars are widely used in online communication, although some people prefer to post a photograph or real image of themself online to promote to others an awareness of how they look. By choosing to use avatars, both client and practitioner are susceptible to preferences and interpretation of the other party which can influence how they are perceived in the online relationship. Some clients may elect to change their avatar frequently dependent on mood, interests, or other factors. All such use of online persona imagery can provide insight into the person and have an impact on the overall relationship.

In an article in *Times Online*, Parsons (2007) defined his experience of interacting online whilst using an avatar as a known reality of communicating with another person through his keyboard. During this experience, he felt the shared use of avatars provided visual digital puppets which interacted through something he defines as a masking game. Such an interpretation suggests that adopting a multi-layered or disguised online avatar can provide protection from being seen openly by others when preferred. Within the context of online supportive interactions, this point may be particularly pertinent where a person feels reticent in revealing aspects of themselves, or is seeking to gain support with personal issues which would feel too exposing if presented in a face-to-face setting. Using an avatar as a form of online identity could provide a 'security blanket' which places the actual person at a distance. This could be interpreted as putting forward an alter ego to a practitioner, a shield, or a representation which is not directly connected to them as a person for the benefit of emotional protection or as a tool further to maintain anonymity.

There can be benefits and disadvantages to assuming an avatar identity, or including a photographic image of oneself, either in the context of being a practitioner or client. From a client perspective, the choice of avatar could increase their sense of power and create hierarchies in group contexts (Jordan, 1999). Where it is apparent that such use is impacting on the dynamics of the online relationship and the potential outcome in a negative manner, it would be relevant for the practitioner to explore this with the client to ascertain the rationale behind adopting an avatar and highlighting the manner in which this is influencing the relationship.

E X E R C I S E   2 . 3

USING AVATARS

Avatars can be used by companies to provide an image for consumers which they hope will be beneficial in bringing custom to the organisation. Consider which company avatars you are familiar with and how they evoke a positive or negative response within you. Think about what is present in the avatar that generates such responses. What do you feel it tells you about the company and the potential for you to feel comfortable in engaging in a consumer relationship with them?

Take this exercise one stage further by considering what you might choose as a personal online avatar to portray a representation of yourself. Reflect upon what it is about the avatar that shows others who you are, or aspects of how you would like to be represented. How might other online practitioners and clients interpret your avatar?

Establishing an online relationship

Just as in a face-to-face interaction, relating to another person in online work requires time and effort from both parties to establish a relationship where there are helpful and meaningful electronic exchanges, as well as an environment where the client experiences a sense of rapport and trust with the practitioner.

An example of this initial forming of the relationship can be illustrated by considering a scenario where a support network receives an enquiry from a client for a first meeting in a face-to-face context with the intention of forming a continuing supportive or therapeutic relationship. Initially, there will be a process of information gathering in order to identify what support is required and how best to achieve a satisfactory outcome for the client. The initial meeting may be constructed on a more superficial relational level whilst an assessment is completed. During this process, both the facilitator and client will begin a process of determining whether they are able to interact on a level which can provide both parties with sufficient 'engagement' to complete the focus of the work together. Where there is the facility for an ongoing relationship to be developed, there is more opportunity to gain a sense of how the client's internal frame of reference is constructed and provides the online helper with a forum to become more in tune with a client's writing and individual communication style. Anthony (2000) defines this process within online working as a platform for reflecting and emulating a client's world and therefore facilitating therapeutic movement.

Box 2.1*   Simulated client example – Sam

Julie receives an email reply from Sam where she illustrates the issues that she wishes to bring to counselling, in conjunction with returning her client agreement and information requested by Julie. The relational element of the email is more distinct, although still indicating an aspect of reservation from the client in engaging on a personal level with the counsellor.

(Continued)

(Continued)

Julie is unperturbed by this during such an early stage of the online relationship and takes time to consider how she could offer both explicit and non-explicit reassurances to the client in her reply. She concludes that focusing on demonstrating empathy and full attention to the client's presenting issues will provide greater reassurance to Sam, that she could gain a positive experience from further exchanges with the counsellor, whilst also encouraging the development of an online relationship.

The necessary conditions for establishing and developing an online relationship

As a therapist, I work within an integrated model of humanistic theoretical orientation, with a predominant emphasis on utilising psychodynamic practice in conjunction with person-centred core conditions. Within this framework, a key feature in establishing a relationship with the client lies in providing a therapeutic space where they feel safe and are able to explore personal issues in a safe environment and where they do not feel judged or affected by any personal bias that I may hold, and this is paramount to facilitating the therapeutic process. A commitment to be fully empathic with any issues presented within the context of a face-to-face or online interaction and being congruent in responses consolidates the client's experience of feeling understood, valued, and not judged. These factors are integral to the building of a therapeutic alliance with clients. Natiello (2002) stipulates that a crucial requirement of an authentic, connected, therapeutic relationship requires empathy and non-judgmental understanding being present at the onset, in order to establish and connect a therapist and client in a therapeutic alliance.

When working online with clients, the practitioner should strive to establish the same level of engagement at the onset of the interaction as would be evident within a face-to-face environment. The environmental differences in working online are immediately apparent as a client does not visit an office to participate in a meeting, as they engage in contact whilst separated from physical representations of the counselling work environment. This factor will undoubtedly hold the potential to contribute positively in providing a more neutral setting for the work to take place and offer a greater sense of empowerment for a client. As the client is likely to be using either a personal location or more public place to make contact with the online helper, it is necessary to inform clients of the need to take steps to ensure their privacy regarding confidentiality of the content of an online interaction. Where a client is unable to feel relaxed and free to discuss issues whilst at their chosen location, a practitioner should offer support and guidance in locating a more appropriate place from which to interact online. This would usually be catered for naturally within a face-to-face interaction within the premises of the professional, providing support and privacy to a client. The online practitioner cannot make the assumption that a client is interacting from within an environment where they are free from disturbance or risk of compromise to safety or security of information disclosed. An example of this might be a client who seeks support regarding domestic violence and does not have access to resources outside of their home in order to interact with a practitioner. It is the responsibility of the practitioner or organisation offering an online service to provide information and guidance to clients regarding security and privacy either via their website or electronic resources available to clients from their website.

The practicalities of developing an online relationship

The practical requirements of seeking to develop an online relationship with a client hold considerable similarity to that which is evident within a professional face-to-face supportive relationship. When referring to practical considerations, which are relevant aspects of developing a professional therapeutic face-to-face relationship, the following points would be particularly pertinent and are transferable to online working (the points are not listed in order of priority):

- Adopting an assessment process.
- Agreeing a contract for the working arrangements which relate to an ethical and supportive relationship, prior to commencing sessions.
- Providing information regarding the extent of confidentiality within the relationship.
- Providing access to client resources which offer guidelines and support relating to online interaction and professional relationships, including information relating to security and privacy of online interaction and data storage.
- Consistency in the professional manner and model of supportive interaction.
- Reliability of the practitioner: giving adequate notification of pending absences due to holidays, and so on, where cancellations are necessary, informing clients appropriately, being punctual and prepared for a session.
- Accessibility of the practitioner: providing alternative contact details to clients in the event of a technology difficulty or unexpected absences of the practitioner.
- Facilitating a sense of containment for clients where difficult emotions or experiences and memories are recalled.
- Holding the information content of sessions with sufficient fluency that it can later be recalled, as required, to assist in an exploration of subsequent material presented by a client.
- Maintaining appropriate professional boundaries.

Variations in areas of professional practice will necessitate consideration to specific practicalities and responsibilities within the area of specialism. It is the responsibility of the practitioner and individual organisations to consider this prior to offering a service to clients.

E X E R C I S E   2 . 4

REASSURING THE CLIENT

Using the information from the simulated client example provided within Box 2.1, consider how you would offer both explicit and non-explicit reassurances in the process of seeking to establish trust and rapport with a client.

E X E R C I S E   2 . 5

PRACTICALITIES TO CONSIDER

Consider the additional practical requirements and responsibilities in your area of professional practice that could influence the potential for developing and maintaining effective and ethical online relationships with clients.

The initial online interaction

Where applicable, following an assessment process, the initial online meeting between practitioner and service user will begin to provide an increased sense for both parties of whether the relationship has the potential to meet the individual needs of the client. Both parties will be actively assessing whether the communication feels comfortable and sufficiently fluid to enable the depth of interaction to fulfil the purpose of the relationship. During a first meeting, it is beneficial to explore with the client the level of comfort they have with interacting online, whilst also discussing the client's confidence with using keyboard skills. Often clients who seek out online support are familiar with computer-mediated technology, keyboard skills, and so on, and are relaxed within forum and chat mediums such as MSN Messenger. Where a level of comfort and familiarity is not evident, it can adversely impact upon the potential for the relationship. By establishing the level of familiarity that a client has with online interaction and computer use at the onset, the practitioner should gain an increased awareness of how best to promote and develop an online relationship with the client, or assist with a referral to a more appropriate means of support where required.

When meeting a client in a face-to-face context, the practitioner will begin to note the style of communication and the variation in language usage which the client possesses. This can be as evident within online working, as each client will 'present' through written narrative in a unique manner which in itself gives the opportunity for the practitioner to consider how best to engage the client. Each online client will present with variables in their style of communication, and even though they may be subtle, there will be unique aspects to the style which provide an opportunity to reflect on how to develop an online dialogue with the client that will assist in developing the relationship. Noting such aspects of the expression will provide the practitioner with the opportunity to consider how best to engage clients and provide reassurances that they are 'in tune' and actively seeking to develop the relationship.

Case example 2.1

Initial communication with a confident client

Practitioner: Hello Mark. Thank you for contacting me for support …. Can we just check a few details before we begin our meeting today?

Mark: Yep that's ok with me. Ask away!

Practitioner: I just wanted to check if you were familiar with seeking support online and if you are comfortable with using a computer?

Mark: I use chat forums a lot and I use the computer for work so I'm ok thanks

Practitioner: Okay. Thank you. It sounds as though you feel comfortable with seeking support online and are used to interacting with others in this way. Perhaps we can begin by you telling me about the personal circumstances which have brought you to our service?

Mark: A friend suggested I get some help as I've got into debt. Living beyond my means-credit cards and that kind of thing

---

Case example 2.2

Initial communication with a less confident client

Practitioner: Hello Jodi. Thank you for contacting me for support …… Can we just check a few details before we begin our meeting today?

Jodi: Hello. Yes that's fine.

Practitioner: I just wanted to check if you were familiar with seeking support online and if you are comfortable with using a computer?

Jodi: This is all new to me so it feels different to how I'd usually get help with things. But I'm okay with using the computer.

Practitioner: Okay. Thank you. It sounds as though you may feel a little unsure about seeking support online. If there is anything that crops up which you feel unclear about please ask me to explain. Towards the end of our meeting today we can also spend some time talking about how this has felt and discuss what you would find helpful next time…. Perhaps we can begin by you telling me about the personal circumstances which have brought you to our service?

Jodi: Okay. Thank you. That would be good as I am feeling a little nervous about how it will be. I need some help with my relationships as I always end up feeling let down by partners. Not sure why though. I think maybe I don't talk enough about my feelings.

Reflecting upon the practitioner's opening greeting within Case examples 2.1 and 2.2, as an online practitioner myself, I would begin to hold a sense of the person I am communicating with from the introductions in the first meeting. The written communication style, word use, and abbreviations used by a client also provide insight into how to adapt one's own communication style to provide the opportunity to develop the online relationship in a positive way. This begins the process of 'online symbiosis' with a client, which is necessary in establishing and building a relationship where a client feels supported, understood, and valued by the practitioner.

Reflecting upon the client's opening greeting

You may have noted that in Case example 2.1, the client who has a relaxed manner uses some abbreviation in his replies. It provides the practitioner with a sense that this is a client who has an informal style in his communication and has a certain air of confidence, both in himself and also in using online interaction. This may, of course, only be an initial impression as a client may at first portray an air of confidence but subsequently move on to displaying more vulnerable aspects of themselves when feeling more relaxed within the relationship.

In Case example 2.2, the practitioner begins the session with the same opening greeting and the client responds with a more formal reply. It can be difficult when first beginning an online interaction to determine how to open the dialogue, as a formal greeting may initially leave a client feeling that they are inhibited by this, just as an informal greeting may create a sense for the client that the practitioner is too familiar at such an early stage of the online interaction. It is beneficial to open with a greeting such as 'Hello' or 'Dear' if using email communication, and subsequently follow the client's lead in their individual preference of greeting style. Where an ongoing relationship is established, a client will often become more at ease and adjust their greeting and communication style within sessions. Where this does not occur, it provides an indication to the practitioner that the client is either not comfortable with interacting online, is feeling a sense of apprehension with the process or the practitioner, or is generally more formal when communicating with others on a personal and professional level. Such aspects provide insight which can inform the therapeutic nature of the interaction and the potential to develop the online relationship.

Variations in communication style within initial asynchronous communication

When working online within an asynchronous context, there will be similarities to those identified in Case examples 2.1 and 2.2.

Although the exchange of dialogue will not be in real time, the manner in which a practitioner and client respond to each other is important in determining the potential for a presence to be established by both parties and to begin the process of developing an online relationship. Within asynchronous communication, there is not the same opportunity to seek clarification or address misunderstandings as they occur; also, a sense of spontaneity can be lost which may have an impact on the developing relationship. It is important to invite discussion with clients where there appears to have been a misunderstanding, and from the onset of both synchronous and asynchronous communication to have highlighted the potential for misunderstandings to occur in online relationships, whilst also extending the offer for clients to seek clarification where required, and vice versa on behalf of the practitioner. Some practitioners and clients may feel they are one step further removed from each other when not interacting in 'real time'. There is also the factor of time delay to be considered as misinterpretations can become amplified if they are not addressed as they occur. Seeking clarification and resolving misunderstandings through asynchronous communication may feel less threatening for some clients, whilst also providing a sense of being able to express their feelings more openly. This in itself could allow a client to become more fully engaged in the relationship and promote greater confidence in being able to express negative feelings within a synchronous online environment, due to holding sufficient trust in the developing relationship that such articulation will not destroy the positive qualities of the developing rapport.

When I refer to negative feeling expression, I am not condoning the use of inappropriate or disrespectful narrative from a client, more so referring to where a client feels able to explicitly convey constructive negative feelings.

Further guidance on managing misunderstandings and conflict can be found in Chapter 5.

⒠⒲⒠⒭⒞⒤⒮⒠ ⒉.⒍

STYLE OF COMMUNICATION

How did you experience the communication and relational style of Case examples 2.1 and 2.2? Consider your natural style of engaging with others and replace the practitioner interventions with alternatives which reflect your personally preferred style.

The impact of opening and closing greetings on the potential for developing and maintaining an online relationship

Some clients do not use greetings or sign-offs at the beginning and end of their online communication. When inviting a client to explore why they have adopted this practice, they may indicate a preference to omit such greetings within personal face-to-face interactions and therefore did not consider it relevant to use them in an online context. Such an absence of greetings and sign-offs directly impacts on the forming of an online relationship and can feel very impersonal and negating of the person receiving the communication.

This may be a communication style that some clients use when interacting with peers, almost as if acknowledgement of each other happens as a 'given', as opposed to being explicitly expressed. With the nature of online communication and resulting relationships being more remote than face-to-face parallels, it is pertinent that both practitioner and client open and close communication with explicit acknowledgements to each party. Failure to engage with this element of the online relationship, or to explore the rationale for not engaging with it, could have a direct impact on the success and depth of the relationship.

EXERCISE   2.7

OPENING AND CLOSING STYLES

Reflect upon your personal opening and closing style within online interaction, and those of others you communicate with. Consider how this assists the intended intonation of your online exchange, and how this may be experienced by the recipient.

Environmental, personal, and technological factors which influence the potential to demonstrate interest and attention when interacting online

Environmental and personal factors

A primary consideration in an online practitioner demonstrating interest and attention to their clients emanates from the environment they are working in and their attention to creating a work space where they are not influenced by personal and external distractions.

The term 'bracketing' is a familiar expression in counsellor training programmes. It is used to describe the process where a practitioner clears their mind of any personal material prior to and during a session with a client. The benefits of this are that the listener is in a position to be fully present with a client and not influenced by any external personal material which could affect the ability to engage with the client and focus on the content within a session. This process requires adaptation when communicating online (Bayne et al., 1999). Other considerations include ensuring that the session will not be disrupted and the setting of a face-to-face meeting being private and providing a space without distraction for both practitioner and client. There may be an assumption that in the context of online support, a practitioner could work within a more informal environment to that of a face-to-face interaction. If an online practitioner is to provide the level of professionalism required to engage clients and focus on developing a strong online relationship, the work environment should emulate that of a face-to-face meeting in so much as they are free from distractions and are fully engaged whilst providing an online session or reply to a client. Similarly, an online client or service user may feel that they are able to adopt a more relaxed approach whilst interacting online with a practitioner, and this may lead to a meeting being disrupted by a client answering the phone or being disturbed by visitors (including those who make contact with a client through email or synchronous communication) whilst the client is actively engaged in synchronous discussion. This may not be apparent if the interaction takes place through asynchronous communication. Such interruptions can adversely affect the flow of a synchronous meeting and generate annoyance or distractions which may impact on the outcome of the meeting and the ability to maintain an effective online presence. It is advisable to establish certain boundaries with clients at the onset, or provide written guidelines outlining the difficulties encountered when meetings are disrupted and the implications of this. Where continued interruptions occur that can be prevented, it is relevant for the practitioner to discuss this with the client and seek a positive way forward in resolving such distractions.

EXERCISE 2.8

Consider how you will ensure that online appointments with clients are not disrupted by both external and personal influences which may arise. When considering the potential factors which may cause disruption, how would you introduce the discussion of prioritising work commitments as a feature?

Technological factors affecting the potential to demonstrate interest and attention

Technology failure may be an issue that affects both the practitioner and client during an online interaction or synchronous exchange of information. If the electronic resources utilised by either party are faulty or prone to interruptions which affect the flow and continuation of a session, this will affect both parties' ability to engage sufficiently to maintain interest and develop the online relationship.

If this occurs during an online interaction and cannot be resolved, it is advisable to suggest an alternative medium such as asynchronous working until the difficulty is rectified. Where a resolution cannot be found, it is beneficial to suggest alternative arrangements, which might include referral to a face-to-face service. Where occurring during an established online relationship, an appropriate closure should be sought prior to onward referral.

The quality of the equipment the online practitioner uses for their work will be an obvious factor that can influence interaction and the online relationship. It is therefore vital to ensure that equipment used is of a good condition and promotes the level of service offered. For example, a computer with a flickering screen will not only lead to frustration on the part of the practitioner, but also reduce the ability to communicate with a client.

Forming a physical perspective of an online client

It can be beneficial when working online with clients to have a visual image in mind of the person you are interacting with. Such images can be formed from a photograph or an avatar used by a client to illustrate themself as an individual. There are occasions where this is not used by a client and may not be necessary, as the client's image is primarily influenced and developed through:

- all facets of how the client presents material
- feeling expression
- individual writing style
- font and colour adaptations
- content of the online communication
- memories recalled
- any apparent personalised content conveyed through their communication.

Holding an image can serve as an advantage of personalising the interaction with the client, whilst also assisting in the development of the online relationship with a client. When discussing with professional colleagues how they would define their 'experiencing' of clients and the presenting material, in the context of face-to-face therapeutic relationships, and how they subsequently utilise this to inform and enhance their insight and empathy to the client, there are some who say they naturally use imagery to gain empathy whilst others refer to experiencing clients in a physical sensory context which subsequently informs their insight, responses, and overall nature of the work. You may wish to consider how you achieve this within your face-to-face interactions and how this might be transferred across to online practice.

With the medium of online counselling being remote, it is particularly pertinent when forming a relationship that a practitioner consciously forms an image and physical perspective of the online client. Failure to engage with this process could result in depersonalising the interaction and forming only a superficial relationship, which would be of obvious detriment to the interaction and to the client. Where an online practitioner does not have an ongoing relationship with a client due to the circumstances of their work setting, there may be limitations on the ability to develop a detailed image of a client. Where this is the case, it is still advantageous to hold a representation, as failure to do so can impair the quality of the interaction and the efficacy of the service provided.

In instances where a practitioner has difficulty in forming an image or internalised perspective of a client, this may be due to resistance on the part of the client to reveal themselves or that they are interacting on a factual level without personalised mannerisms or relational qualities being included. Where the nature of the online relationship necessitates a more in-depth understanding of the client and material presented within the interactions, the online practitioner should endeavour to encourage a greater level of personal presence to assist in developing a physical perspective of the client and therefore improve the quality of the online relationship.

Gaining a physical perspective of a client is directly relevant in the forming and development of an online relationship, and I would invite you to reflect on how you engage with others when a physical absence is not evident in other contexts. The following exercise may assist with developing your insight into this point.

EXERCISE 2.9

PHYSICAL PERSPECTIVE

As an illustration of how we form a relationship with an individual in a fictional perspective, I would ask that you take some time to reflect upon a character in a novel that you felt engaged with and who seemed to 'come to life' for you through the manner in which the author had portrayed them. What was present in the written portrayal of a character that brought them to life for you and helped with the process of engagement?

Taking this a step further, consider how the quality of your relationship with the character could have been further enhanced by the author and the key aspects that would have facilitated this process.

You may feel that using a fictional example to illustrate this point is somewhat distanced from interacting with a real person; if this is the case, you might want to complete the exercise using an autobiography as an example and consider how you engaged with the writer of the text when you have not met them in a physical setting.

I have placed particular emphasis on discussing in this section how a practitioner develops a physical perspective of a client to assist in developing an online relationship. The online practitioner is, without a doubt, key to influencing and affecting the relational qualities of online interaction and relationships, and should therefore pay due attention to how the practitioner's own physical perspective is conveyed to clients in order to promote engagement and facilitate a positive outcome.

Helping clients to help themselves – problem solving

I have included problem solving within this chapter as I believe the nature of online communication creates a different emphasis in how support is explored and provided when assisting clients to help themselves. Consequently, this can impact directly on the quality and dynamics within the online relationship if due consideration is not given to how this is aided by the practitioner. In all instances, it is preferable that clients are provided with non-directive interventions which encourage a process of developing innate problem-solving skills (Kraus et al., 2004).

I am basing the context of this process within interactions where the practitioner is encouraging a client to develop problem-solving skills as opposed to settings where the practitioner provides advice and support within a professional requirement of their employment remit, that is, a therapeutic setting rather than an information and advice service. When working online, the time spent communicating between practitioner and client is reduced compared to what can be covered in a one-hour face-to-face meeting, due to the content being written as opposed to verbal dialogue. This is more apparent in a synchronous exchange as time is taken in writing, whilst also reflecting on the respondent's text, as opposed to purely reflecting and subsequently verbalising thoughts and responses, as occurs in a face-to-face dialogue. The process of encouraging a client to engage with problem solving elicited from their own process of insight and natural problem-solving skills, as opposed to being directed from the practitioner, requires particular consideration within the setting of online working, as failure to do so can directly impact on the dynamics within the relationship and move it away from a mutual stance to one which is directed by the practitioner and does not promote autonomy within the client. This factor is apparent primarily by the reduction in time available to allow a more client-led approach and for consideration in how a client can approach a problem without being unduly guided by the practitioner. The pressure of time and absence of body language and physical inferences used by a practitioner and client to indicate that they are sharing or allocating responsibility to the other party for finding a resolution to a problem can make the process of assisting a client in problem solving more complex.

The following examples may help to clarify how the role of the practitioner may vary in the context of online interaction and face-to-face practice, and subsequently the practicalities of problem solving with clients, whilst also maintaining an appropriate presence and online relationship.

Case example 2.3

Face-to-face problem solving

Abdul is employed as a part-time sessional counsellor in an FE college. He works face-to-face with clients who self-refer, or have been referred to the service due to academic issues influenced by personal circumstances such as anxiety or stress. Abdul is aware that his main remit is to help clients maintain their academic study whilst also offering therapeutic support to alleviate the presenting symptoms which are inhibiting progress within the academic context.

His service offers six sessions to clients (equivalent of five hours in actual time, based upon a 50-minute counselling session) to build a relationship and work together in finding a resolution to the presenting issues. Although this may bring its own pressure due to limitation of sessions, Abdul has the advantage of his client being physically present and as such benefits from visual and auditory cues, alongside body language nuances, which will assist him in allowing the client to take the lead in the process of gaining personal insight and problem solving. He also has the advantage of visual indicators enabling him to stand back and allow reflection by the client. These factors will potentially improve the quality of the relationship, whilst also allowing problem solving to be facilitated within the natural flow of the sessions, using face-to-face counselling skills to encourage his clients to be proactive in problem solving.

Where clients present in sessions as resistant to change or gaining personal insight, Abdul utilises his own and his clients' body language, visual expression, and incidents of silence to assist in empowering a client to be proactive in problem solving. Abdul may also draw upon information sheets and reference points that he can offer to clients which assist in providing further options to resolve difficulties.

Case example 2.4

Online problem solving

Abdul is also employed in a university counselling service as a part-time online counsellor. His remit is the same as given in Example 2.3, but his client base is sourced from online work.

He works with clients for six sessions and as such has six actual hours in which to engage with clients either synchronously or via email exchanges. The actual time and flow of sessions is minimised due to the factors previously indicated. As a result, Abdul has only the textual information and exchanges with a client, alongside how he has developed the relationship with the client when problem solving during the course of the online sessions. In face-to-face encounters, he has time to sit back and consider what is taking place within his interaction and glean some indication from his client's body language and other visual and auditory expression. He will not have the same access during online interactions. When working in a synchronous exchange with clients, he may also experience a sense of pressure to 'cut to the chase', which he doesn't experience in face-to-face work, as the exchanges between himself and the client are reduced by having to consider and type his response whilst maintaining engagement with the client and the presenting issue. As a result of these influences, there will be a process of Abdul having to be more concise and to the point when responding to online clients, whilst also ensuring that he does not eradicate or reduce the important process of allowing clients to develop their own problem-solving skills. This is developed over a period of time by attending to the structure and content of the written narrative he conveys to clients in both synchronous and asynchronous exchanges.

Abdul has adapted his face-to-face counselling skills into a framework that translates appropriately to online counselling skills in a manner which does not impede the process of empowering clients in problem solving, whilst also paying attention to maintaining balance within the relationship.

EXERCISE 2.10

PROBLEM SOLVING IN AN ONLINE CONTEXT

Using the following scenario, consider how your response in assisting a client with problem solving in an online interaction may differ from a face-to-face meeting. You may like to try this exercise with a partner where you each take a turn in assuming the two roles within the scenario and alternate between face-to-face interactions and communicating synchronously or asynchronously online. Upon completion of the exercise, discuss any apparent skills variation that occur when using the two mediums in supporting the client with problem solving, whilst also considering how you feel this had influenced your sense of presence as an online practitioner and the overall quality of the relationship.

Scenario: A middle-aged male approaches your service for support with work-related stress. You have a one-hour meeting with him in which he would like to discuss the following:

a) To find a way to discuss work priorities with his manager in order to reduce his stress levels.
b) To consider ways in which he can relax in his leisure time, as opposed to spending much of his spare time worrying about his work situation.
c) To discuss the impact of his current stress levels on his long-term relationship, and explore ways to restore a good level of harmony with his partner.

Summary

This chapter has discussed the relevance of presence in an online relationship and how this dynamic can assist in developing and maintaining that relationship. The manner in which this is experienced by a practitioner and developed within an online relationship is realised through the practical application of working online with clients. I hope that the examples and exercises provided have assisted in developing this intuition for you as the reader. The process of developing a relationship with an online client is integral to there being a positive outcome in providing online support to clients.

There will be variations in the skills level and communication styles possessed by clients when seeking online support, and these factors will influence the potential for forming and maintaining both a positive online relationship and the potential for a successful outcome.

The role of the online practitioner is to promote a sense of online presence in themselves and their clients whilst also supporting the establishment of a productive and positive online relationship and experience for their clients.

Points for consideration

- How will you facilitate positive client outcomes given the absence of visual and auditory cues to assist with the process?
- What assessment procedures will you adopt to determine client skill levels in using computer-mediated technology and their ability to communicate effectively through online interactions?
- How might differences in adopted avatars vary within gender orientation and other aspects of difference and diversity?
- What practical experience do you possess in assisting clients with problem solving, and how will you transfer this to online interactions with clients?

References

Anthony, K. (2000) 'Counselling in Cyberspace', *Counselling*, 11 (10): 625–7.

Bayne, R., Norton, I., Merry, T., Noyes, E. and McMahon, G. (1999) *The Counsellor's Handbook*, 2nd edition. Cheltenham: Nelson Thornes.

Cooper, W. (2002) 'Information technology and internet culture', *Journal of Virtual Environments*, 6 (1). Available at www.brandeis.edu/pubs/jove/index.html.

Hamburger, Y. (2005) *The Social Net: Understanding Human Behaviour in Cyberspace*. New York: Oxford University Press. p. 29.

Jordon, T. (1999) *Cyberpower: The Culture and Politics*. London: Routledge. p. 81.

Kraus, R., Zack, J. and Stricker, G. (2004) *Online Counselling: A Handbook for Mental Health Professionals*. San Diego, CA: Elsevier/Academic Press. p. 195.

Nakamura, L. (2002) *Cybertypes: Race, Ethnicity, and Identity on the Internet*. London: Routledge. p. 54.

Natiello, P. (2002) *The Person-Centred Approach: A Passionate Presence*. Ross-on-Wye: PCCS Books. p. 31.

Nowak, K.L. and Rauh, C. (2005) 'The influence of the avatar on online perceptions of anthropomorphism, androgyny, credibility, homophily, and attraction', *Journal of Computer-Mediated Communication*, 11 (1). Available at http://jcmc.indiana.edu/vol11/issue1/nowak.html.

Parsons, M. (2007) 'Things I have learnt from my Avatar: Avatar-based communication – or ABC to those in the know – has much to teach us about living in a virtual world', *Times Online*, 20 July. Available at http://technology.timesonline.co.uk/tol/news/tech_and_web/gadgets_and_gaming/virtual_worlds/article2111182.ece.

Prado, S. and Meyer, S.B. (2004) *Evaluation of the Working Alliance in Asynchronous Therapy via the Internet*. Sao Paulo: University of Sao Paulo. Available at www.psico.net/arquivos.

Rogers, C.R. (1980) *A Way of Being*. Boston, MD: Houghton Mifflin. p. 129.

Suler, J. (1997) *Psychological Dynamics of Online Synhronous Conversations in Text-Driven Chat Environments*. Available at www.rider.edu/users/suler/psycyber/texttalk.html.

Suler J. (2003) *The Psychology of Cyberspace: E-mail Communication and Relationships*. Available at www.rider.edu/~suler/psycyber/presence.html.

Whitmore, D. (2004) *Psychosynthesis Counselling in Action*. London: Sage. p. 41.

Further reading, references, resources, and skill development activities relating to the subject matter within this chapter can be sourced via the companion website to this book.

3 ONLINE EXPRESSION

Online counselling skills presented in this chapter:

- Online empathy
- Online feeling expression
- Responding to feelings during computer-mediated interactions
- Disinhibition in online expression
- The use of acronyms and emoticons

Exercises and vignettes are included within this chapter, demonstrating the skills in practice and encouraging thought on the subject matter discussed.

This chapter discusses the skills of online empathy and the aptitudes required to identify and work with feelings which are explicitly expressed, unexpressed, and feelings which are more obscure in an online context. In conjunction with resistance and non-verbal cues, the evidence of such feeling expression will often be 'hidden' within the text, or at the opposite standpoint signified by the writer using outbursts of **CAPITALS WITH BOLD TEXT and the use of exclamation marks !!!!!**

If you are familiar with working with clients in a face-to-face context, you will be tuned to evident visual and verbal signals which can assist in encouraging a client to identify and work with their feelings. Within such a context, there is also the advantage of witnessing body language inconsistencies that can draw attention to unexpressed feeling and internal conflict. When engaging with clients using computer-mediated communication (CMC), such auditory and visual cues will be less apparent due to both parties not having the benefit of actual person-to-person contact to assist in this process. The online practitioner is required to consider how feelings may be conveyed in a different manner to that which is encountered within face-to-face interactions, and reflect upon the content of client online narrative accordingly (Suler, 2003).

Online empathy

Empathy is a key skill in both online and face-to-face supportive interventions, and professional counselling skills practice. Successful online empathy is achieved in a dual process of conveying empathic accuracy, in conjunction with a supportive response. Feng et al. (2003) highlight empathy as a key element in the success of online web board discussion groups.

Preece (1998) and Manney (2006) hold an opposing view, stating that written narrative and storytelling hold the highest potential to activate another's empathy. Empathic accuracy and responses provided by practitioners have a direct impact upon the level of trust experienced by online clients (Feng et al., 2003).

With such distinct variations of opinion in mind, I hope this section of the chapter provides a platform for you to determine the potential for gaining online empathy.

Gaining empathy of clients' presenting issues and the true experiencing of clients' inner worlds is paramount to the process of a practitioner being able to sit alongside clients in a manner where they identify and understand the person's experiences and feelings. In the context of computer-mediated interactions, this requires specific skills adaptation due to apparent restrictions in having access to visual, audio, and physical indicators that assist the process of acquiring empathic understanding. Without practitioners actively seeking to gain empathy in all manners of their clients' presentations and communication, this would result in the interaction becoming a purely narrative exchange and therefore no more effective than an online conversation. Practitioners are reliant on their clients' ability to express themselves and their experiences in a narrative form to enable online empathic understanding.

Feng et al. (2003) emphasise a requirement for practitioners to provide guidelines to their online clients that outline the manner in which they can effectively communicate their experiences and needs and subsequently promote practitioner empathic understanding. Guidelines should be made available to clients prior to commencing online interaction with a practitioner.

Empathic responses during asynchronous exchanges

Where there is an absence of clients providing detailed insight to their presenting issues or needs, a practitioner's skill lies in the process of encouraging a client to be explicit in their online narrative and use of dialogue. This heightens the potential for empathic understanding, in conjunction with promoting the client's sense of the practitioner being attuned and actively seeking to develop the required level of engagement.

When providing clients with guidance in this area, it is important to avoid being overly prescriptive in order that the client is allowed to form the content of their initial, and subsequent, communication without unduly considering the needs of the practitioner. A client should feel that they are the narrator of the content and therefore can freely express themself without overt interference form the practitioner. Finding the balance where a practitioner gains sufficient information to gain empathy without hindering or directing the client is an acquired skill.

Throughout the chapters within Part I of this book, you will have the opportunity to see simulated examples of both synchronous and asynchronous online client exchanges. Such examples contain illustrations of the process where a practitioner seeks to gain empathic understanding, whilst also actively using additional online counselling skills.

Further simulated client examples in Box 3.1 and Box 3.2, using the containing example of Sam from Chapter 1, focus specifically on how a practitioner can seek to increase their empathic understanding during both asynchronous and synchronous online interactions.

Box 3.1*   Sam's second email to the practitioner

Dear Julie,

You asked me to write this second email giving some details about what kind of support I need and a bit of background to myself. I'd like help regarding the relationship I have with my children, particularly my eldest child who is 14. I worry that my eldest doesn't talk to me in the same way she used to. We used to be so close and I never worried about what she might be doing outside of the home or at school, but lately she seems reluctant to talk and even gets angry when I ask about where she's going and what she's doing. I've heard so many worrying things about what teenagers are doing in our area that it's making me think that my daughter's involved in some way. I can't think of any other reason for her behaviour changing. She used to help out at home and even look after her younger brother and sister. Lately she's not interested in the family and doesn't really talk to any of us. I need help to find out what's going on before she gets into trouble.

I am a lone parent and I have a lot of things that I'm responsible for as I don't have a partner or family to help out and talk to. I'm studying for a degree in primary education and I will be beginning my placement next term. This makes me feel more concerned about leaving my daughter as she will have more time to be away from home whilst I'm working in a local school.

I hope you can help.

Sam

Box 3.2* The practitioner's reply to Sam

Dear Sam,

I can hear how concerned you feel about the changes you are noticing in the relationship you have with your daughter, what you feel may be causing this, and your fears regarding her getting into trouble. I have a sense that previously you had the reassurance that all was well with your daughter due to having a close relationship with her. Her recent distancing from you, and the anger she is displaying, is causing you to feel that she may be involved in activities that could be harmful to her. I can hear that her anger towards your questions, regarding what she is doing and where she is going, is leaving you feeling that the communication between you is more difficult, and I sense that you may be experiencing some reservation in pursuing with your questions as a result of this.

There seems to be quite a lot of incidences, which you discuss in your email, where you feel that your daughter is withdrawing from you and her younger brother and sister. I have a sense (although I'm aware that you haven't mentioned this) that not only does this concern you, but it is also causing you to feel that you and your children have lost an aspect of closeness in the relationship with your daughter.

You mention, towards the end of your email, that you are a lone parent and within that context you feel that you don't have others close to you who are available to talk through any problems or concerns you may have regarding your children. I can hear how much of a responsibility this feels for you and how difficult this situation could be, as you are making important decisions alone. I hope that through the support I can offer that you are able to experience the current difficulties as more manageable for you...........

The above section of the practitioner reply to the client within Box 3.2 is focused on offering empathy to all aspects of presented material within the client's initial email. The purpose of this is to focus on providing a response where the client feels the practitioner has heard all the content. The reply provides empathy and understanding in how the client is experiencing her difficulties, whilst encouraging the client to engage in the online relationship. The practitioner is working hard to gain a deeper level of empathy by attempting to consider additional feelings and concerns the client may have, but which have not been explicitly expressed. There is less probing within this exchange than occurs in subsequent emails, as the practitioner wishes to be more attentive to 'listening' and responding in an attempt to engage the client. In the process of seeking to express empathy and gain a deeper level of understanding, the practitioner uses terms similar to those used in a face-to-face supportive interaction. The terms include: I have a sense ..., I'm feeling ..., I can hear ..., It sounds as if ..., and so on. Where an online practitioner is a little unsure of the client's meaning, this can be substituted with the additional wording of: I think I can hear, and so on. When using online empathy skills, there is not the opportunity to see or notice visibly how the client is responding to the empathic responses. It can therefore be helpful when feeling unsure of how the intervention will be received to add a bracketed message for the client as is demonstrated in Box 3.2.

ⒺⓍⒺⓇⒸⒾⓈⒺ   ③.①

EMPATHIC REASSURANCE

Consider how you would reply to the client example provided in Box 3.1.

What features of conveying empathy would you draw upon from your face-to-face and/or your current online exchanges with others to provide reassurances to the client that you are accurately demonstrating empathy and providing a supportive response?

Empathic responses during synchronous exchanges

During synchronous exchanges with clients, there is the advantage of having access to immediacy where the practitioner can encourage further information and clarification from a client to increase their empathic understanding. There is also the immediate opportunity to seek clarification on subject matter and interventions made by either party. The pace of a synchronous session can, on occasion, hinder the process of gaining empathic understanding, as a one-hour synchronous meeting can be experienced as placing additional pressure on both the practitioner and client. This is due to both parties being engaged in forming the cognitive and emotional content of their dialogue, and typing this whilst also reading the replies from the other person on the screen. The content of an online synchronous meeting may be experienced as more limiting and inhibiting. There are distinct advantages to working with clients using both asynchronous and synchronous exchanges. This may promote the potential for gaining empathy, as it is possible to compensate for deficits or barriers evident within each context of CMC.

Ⓔ︎Ⓧ︎Ⓔ︎Ⓡ︎Ⓒ︎Ⓘ︎Ⓢ︎Ⓔ︎   ③.②

EMPATHIC RESPONSES

When considering the scope for empathic responses in both asynchronous and synchronous online contexts, identify which would feel a more comfortable setting for you, and the reasons for your decision.

Online feeling expression

In face-to-face helping interactions, there are visual physical indications, tonal cues, and verbal dialogue which assist the helper to understand a client's form of expression and any variations. Facial expression and body language are a key factor in assisting the understanding of human expression and personal feelings. They are present as an implicit aid for the helper to gain a deeper level of insight and understanding to the issues being presented (Stokoe, 2001). For those who have trained in a professional helping or support capacity, there will have been a focused aspect of training to assist in becoming alert to body language and auditory and tonal cues. They are valuable tools for assisting an understanding of the individual needs of those who are seeking help or support. The absence of a physical presence leaves online practitioners with the task of extending existing counselling competencies, whilst also developing a new range of skills to ensure an insightful level of understanding in online human expression. When working with computer-mediated technology, the online practitioner focuses on the style and content of the material to gain a sense of the client and their individual personality and forms of expression.

The skill of identifying unexpressed feelings when working online is developed by looking for subtle cues which are present within the narrative and encouraging the sender to explore presented material at a deeper level.

As in the context of face-to-face interactions, each online client varies in how they communicate and express themself. It is possible to become familiar with and begin to understand individual 'methods of online feeling expression', and also what deeper emotions may lay beneath the more superficial expression received in a textual format. As the online relationship progresses, a greater level of understanding and feeling expression develops by practitioners being able to sense what lies beyond that which is both explicitly and non-explicitly expressed. At this point, the strength of the online relationship will also hold more potential for the helper to offer challenges without creating defensiveness which could hinder the outcome of the work. Responding to a client outside the offering of empathy and unconditional positive regard, or making an intervention based upon the practitioner's own values, belief system, or personal experiences and not based upon the client's own self-structure and experiences, would be inappropriate and detrimental to the relationship (Tolan, 2003)

Personal forms of online feeling expression

As in all aspects of verbal communication, there is a human tendency towards establishing a repertoire of personal expression. As such, the people who communicate with us regularly begin to recognise our unique representations of emotion and the depth to which we are experiencing them.

Those who interact through electronic mediums can, and do, develop ways of expressing themselves effectively to a depth where feelings are conveyed in a manner which is clear, creative, and understood by the recipient (Zelvin, 2003). Difficulty can arise where a client has a limited verbal emotional vocabulary or is limited in expression of emotion through a non-verbal computer-sourced medium. It may be that you, as facilitator of the online interaction, will offer examples of feeling expression in your conveyance of empathy which can serve as an illustration to clients. Where it becomes apparent that a client does not hold sufficient potential to express themself through CMC, a referral to a face-to-face support service should be discussed with the client.

Therapeutic benefits of feeling expression in the absence of a 'physical presence' when working online

The absence of a practitioner's physical representation can assist with a client being free to work without the same level of shame and guilt which may be apparent for clients in a face-to-face context. Shame and guilt often become apparent when a client reveals something which they are finding difficult to discuss. They will look down or look away, due to the discomfort in maintaining eye contact. There are other feelings which can be difficult to convey and express in the physical presence of another person, often based upon personal history and external dynamics such as social, cultural, gender, family constructs, and so on. CMC can be advantageous as discussion regarding uncomfortable feelings may be experienced in a different manner from face-to-face contexts. This factor places an emphasis on the professional who works with clients online to assist with such disclosures using an approach which is productive, safe, and appropriately 'contained'. This requires an increased sensitivity from the practitioner, due to the absence of a client's physical presence and inability to offer the same reassurances and support adopted during face-to-face exchanges. More frequent checking is required to assess how the client is experiencing their feeling expression, particularly in areas where the client's sense of vulnerability is enhanced, such as a disinhibited response.

Practitioners may encounter clients who have previous experience of self and feeling expression by frequenting online resources such as Facebook, and so on, and positively acknowledge the benefits of doing so. Across a global context in many social platforms, the benefits in online feeling expression are being identified, even to a point of having enhanced potential to self-empathise (Kyung Hee and Haejin, 2007).

🄴🄭🄴🅁🄲🄸🅂🄴   🄳.🄳

FEELING EXPRESSION

What kind of online phrases might you use to check with clients if their expression or revealing of feelings has left them feeling uncomfortable or vulnerable?

How might your email reply differ to the practitioner response provided in Box 3.2 when seeking to clarify issues relating to feeling expression, or the absence of it?

Online expression of feeling

To illustrate how feelings may be identified and explored when working online, take a moment or two to reflect on a letter or email you have received from someone which left you: knowing that the other person was either explicitly expressing a feeling to you; or having read the entire text, you held a sense of what they were conveying, although they did not directly express specific feelings.

When feelings are openly expressed, the recipient can respond or encourage further discussion, holding the potential to pave the way for a deeper understanding and articulation. Where feelings have not been overtly expressed, the recipient may reply to the sender based upon assumptions formed from reading the text of the sender's email or letter and begin to encourage further disclosure of feelings which were not explicitly expressed. Careful consideration should be given to how you convey your initial understanding of non-expressed emotion and feeling. Offer a tentative interpretation and encourage further exploration or clarification from the sender. This point is particularly pertinent in the early stages of online communication and the building of a relationship. Miscommunication or an over-emphasis of interpretation at this point could affect the potential to develop a trusting and congruent online interaction or relationship (Feng et al., 2003).

Online clients may experience a realisation of their feelings following a spontaneous outburst of expression, such as that described within the introduction to this chapter. This can occur in both synchronous and asynchronous communication where clients take advantage of fully 'venting' thoughts regarding an experience, person, or situation. When this occurs, clients may pause for a moment or two after writing expletives in bold and capitals and reflect on what they had written. The client will often follow on with a reflection of how they have reached a realisation of their feelings which they had previously not recognised or acknowledged through their own personal thought process. The practice of writing and expressing oneself in an online context holds the potential to create therapeutic expression and understanding of feelings. With such expression being held in a text format, it also remains undisputed, and this can often be useful for a client when looking back on their online interaction as a tool for remembering how they felt about specific incidents which were disclosed. Seeing written therapeutic expression, and writing it oneself, can feel more profound and concrete than when verbalising it in a physical context.

EXERCISE 3.4

CREATING AN ONLINE NARRATIVE

Recall a situation which has left you feeling troubled or uneasy. Take some time to type details of the event using a Word document or blank email without pausing to consider what you have written. I would suggest that you spend at least 30 minutes on completing the exercise, or longer if needed. When completed, read back through the text and reflect upon how you have expressed the event and what feelings arose naturally. Take a further moment or two to consider what, if any, feelings were not explicitly conveyed.

If you have the chance to work in pairs, there is the benefit of completing this exercise in an online context with the typed text sent to your partner as an email. This provides the opportunity of seeing the content in an electronic form and sharing your thoughts and responses regarding the expression within the emails.

Considerations for feeling expression in an online context

When receiving synchronous online communication, the recipient does not know if the text was edited or amended prior to being sent. This will be worth noting, as you may not receive the initial written account conveyed by a client. There may have been adjustments made as the content was reviewed. When working in a synchronous context, this would not occur in the same manner, as there is a limited opportunity to edit text before 'releasing' it onto the shared communication board. Within the context of both asynchronous and synchronous CMC, there may be content which has been omitted, either consciously or unconsciously. Often this can be identified through further exploration or reflection on the typed narrative intonation.

Asynchronous communication provides the opportunity for both the sender and recipient to have the advantage of a 'zone of reflection' where spontaneous responses can be constructed and later reviewed prior to the actual sending of the email (Suler, 2004a). The recipient of an email communication may have a sense that the creator of the email has amended the content due to an evident lack of spontaneity and expression of feeling. As within face-to-face interactions, spontaneity has a useful place in assisting the exploration of online feelings and their expression, in conjunction with creating a more reflective process where greater consideration to conscious and unconscious feelings becomes apparent.

EXERCISE　3.5

ZONE OF REFLECTION

What do you consider to be the advantages/disadvantages in having a 'zone of reflection' prior to constructing a response? How might this differ for both yourself and online clients?

Identifying feelings

Within a face-to-face interaction, feelings are often identified by listening to the client whilst observing body language and visual cues. On occasion, feelings may also be highlighted by an inconsistency between what is being spoken and how the speaker reacts when recounting a presented issue. An example of this may be where a client talks about the death of their parent as a very traumatic experience, yet displays no signs of upset or distress when presenting this within a counselling session. Within an online interaction, this inconsistency can be more difficult to identify.

If we consider the example in Box 3.3, we can see how a client expresses themself and the manner in which the potential to explore this further arises. In the example provided, there is an opportunity to reply to the client, and clarification sought regarding the absence in recognition of feelings. There is confusion on the part of the client, as they have the awareness that all is not well but cannot pin-point why they are not functioning on a level they would choose.

Box 3.3*   Sam explores her feelings

Hi

In your last email to me you asked if I could give you some background to my family history. I'm not sure how much I need to say.....but here goes. I am the youngest of four children.....with two brothers and a sister. My parents had me later in life, and my eldest brother was 28 when I arrived. My mum was 48 when I was born, and my father 62. My father died when I was 11 and my mother passed away 2 years ago after battling with breast cancer for a number of years. My sister and brothers seem to have accepted mum dying and just carry on with life and their own families. They managed the financial matters after mum's death and helped me to find some where to live after the family house had been sold. I have my partner who is older than me if I need any support, but he has two young children from his first marriage who take up a lot of his time. When mum died I struggled at first, but I now have a nice place where I live and I mostly get on with life without too many problems. It's just sometimes I feel lonely and can't seem to find the motivation to do the everyday things that I should be doing.............

Having read the example in Box 3.3, you may have formed an opinion of which explicit feelings are present for the client, undisclosed, or currently out of awareness. The client has provided information which helps to gain insight into their family and the relationships with both parents, siblings, and their respective partners. The information is brief and does not indicate specific feelings except for a sense of loneliness, but there are underlying cues which would require further exploration by the respondent.

The initial reading of the email provides a sense of unexpressed feelings and this could be borne in mind for a response to the client, or to refer back to in a subsequent email.

The prominent issues presented within Box 3.3 are the chain of loss and isolation which the writer has experienced. These include:

1. The loss of a father at a young age.
2. The death of her mother through a long illness.

3. The loss of her family home.
4. A sense of distance from her siblings.
5. The potential feeling of isolation experienced by living alone.
6. Feeling displaced by her partner at times, as his children naturally take priority.
7. An absence of feeling supported at times in an emotional context.

Responding to feelings during computer-mediated interactions

Providing a response to feelings expressed within an online context have to be considered in a different manner within both synchronous and asynchronous exchanges, particularly if working within a time-limited framework. There will be the requirement to consider when an appropriate interpretation can be offered regarding expressed and non-expressed feelings, and when it is likely to have most significant impact for the client. Kraus et al. (2004) refer to an evident dynamic within asynchronous communication where written text responses between people can remain suspended until one person initiates a response. The time factor between exchanges can therefore allow a less spontaneous sense of the other's immediate reaction to that which has been written. This also creates the potential to place written words into a suspended arena and individuals not accepting responsibility for what has been expressed. Such a time delay between interactions can also create the potential for either a space to allow intense initial reaction to dissipate, or generate a deepened sense of misunderstanding or conflict. The following preparations, prior to a first session, can assist in synchronous or asynchronous engagement with a client:

- Where the nature of support provided is a one-off interaction, the practitioner would commence the interaction with a statement indicating how misunderstandings may arise and offer the opportunity for the client to seek clarification if this occurs.
- Where a client is accessing ongoing online support, the helping professional provides the client with information prior to commencing an online relationship, which details how misunderstandings may occur and explicitly invites the client to seek clarification if this occurs.

It is beneficial for the practitioner to establish that there may be occasions where they would seek clarification from a client if required.

When responding to the client in Box 3.3, it is important to validate any expressed feelings, gently probing to help identify how the issues impact upon the client, and the resulting feelings that are evoked by their circumstances. This can be achieved by offering empathy and congruence in how the respondent experienced reading the content of the email. An example email reply is illustrated in Box 3.4

Box 3.4 The practitioner's reply to the client email

Dear Sam,

Thank for your reply and for telling me more about your family and current circumstances.

I am so sorry to hear that you have experienced the loss of both of your parents and also your family home. When I read your email I was left unsure regarding how you have felt at the time of your parents' deaths and how you have managed such a series of loss and change within your life. I also wonder how you experience these events in your life currently? You mention in your email that there are times when you feel lonely and there are occasions where you find it hard to motivate yourself towards everyday activities. I have a sense that there are times when you feel weighed down by your situation and find it hard to manage day to day things on your own. I hear that you have had some support from your brothers and sisters, but you feel that they are not affected by your mother's death in the same way that you have been, and still are. It does feel as though you have the support of your partner, but at times this is limited by him having to share his time with his children.................

Affirmation of feelings expressed in an online context

By affirming the client's feelings, it provides the opportunity to bring them to a broader recognition and leaves an opportunity for the client to explore this further in their next email reply. If this was not apparent when receiving a response from the client, it may be relevant to come back to this at a later point by inviting further discussion. In their reply, the practitioner endeavoured to open up areas for the client to begin an exploration of feelings relating to issues regarding their siblings' response to the loss of a parent. This had been indicated by the client as a potential issue which had not been addressed. You may have noted in Box 3.4 that the practitioner offered the opportunity for the client to explore an aspect of their feelings further where they asked: 'I also wonder how you experience these events in your life currently?' By including a question mark at the end of the sentence, it places an emphasis on thoughts which had been held from reading the email and an invitation to the client to respond in their subsequent email reply.

In respect of the client's difficulty with maintaining daily activities, the offering of a mild empathic response, relating to a sense of the client feeling 'weighed down', introduced an opening which could be discussed at a later point by the client. This type of intervention should be offered after careful consideration, as if not presented appropriately this may leave the person feeling misunderstood or judged in some way by the practitioner. It may also be an area of feeling which is out of the client's current awareness, and offering an intervention in this way at an early stage could provide a false sense of the feeling to the client. This may hinder their personal 'experiencing' and interpretation of it.

Contrasts in online feeling expression

Within both synchronous and asynchronous communication, there will be instances where feeling expression is identified by using common or personally adapted techniques, such as the insertion of bracketed text. This signifies where a sense of inner reflection is conveyed and expression of important emotion is highlighted. Collie et al. (2001) define this as 'emotional bracketing'.

This assists the reader in understanding how the feelings are experienced and provides a greater understanding of the writer's inner world and emotions surrounding events or relationships which are recalled. If we take the example from Box 3.3 and extend this to include further emotional expression, it provides an illustration of how a deeper level of insight can be achieved to the client's internal thought processes and the experiencing of feelings.

Box 3.5   Client response using adopted techniques

Hi :-)

............In your last email to me you asked if I could give you some background to my family history. I'm not sure how much I need to say.....but here goes. I am the youngest of four children.....with two brothers and a sister. My parents had me later in life, and my eldest brother was 28 when I arrived. My mum was 48 when I was born, and my father 62. My father died when I was 11 and my mother passed away 2 years ago after battling with breast cancer for a number of years. (feeling sad here as it's reminding me of that time ☹). My sister and brothers seem to have accepted mum dying and just carry on with life and their own families. They managed the financial matters after mum's death and helped me to find some where to live after the family house had been sold. << They're good at practical things like that>>

> I have my partner who is older than me if I need any support, but he has two young children from his first marriage who take up a lot of his time......writing that has made me realise how at times **they take priority over me** (not sure how I feel about that !!)
>
> When mum died I struggled at first, but I now have a nice place where I live and I mostly get on with life without too many problems. It's just sometimes I feel lonely and can't seem to find the motivation to do the everyday things that I should be doing......(shouldn't be feeling this way ... **selfish of me to do that**) ... gosh ... this is hard work :-(................

The key points of online expression contained within the simulated client example in Box 3.5 are:

- The client begins her email with a smiling face to indicate a feeling of warmth towards the service provider.
- The client has used brackets to highlight internal thought processes and the emotions evoked by the thoughts.
- The client has used << >> to emphasise a personal belief and indicate a sense that the belief is solid and undisputed.
- Bold lettering is introduced to indicate the depth of how the client feels in relation to her partner's children being given priority over her.
- Bold lettering is used again towards the end of the email to give a judgmental tone in response to her behaviour.
- The use of extended full stops accentuate breaks in a thought or expression process and ends this with an unhappy face emoticon to convey a further illustration of the impact of exploring the issues contained within the email.

EXERCISE 3.6

DEVELOPING ONLINE FEELING EXPRESSION

Take the example from Box 3.3 and adapt it further by adding a deeper reflection on the feelings expressed in the content of your typed text. You may wish to develop the examples provided in Box 3.5, or create your own adaptations of online feeling expression.

The exercise can be completed on your own or by sharing with a partner. Discuss how it felt to express the level of emotional content of the recalled event within the initial email at a further depth in the subsequent email.

Disinhibition in online expression

When first communicating and providing information online, clients may feel apprehensive in sharing information and personal emotion. Online communication opens up increased potential for transference and projection as there is more left unknown about who we are communicating with. Both client and practitioner may develop a 'fantasy' image of the other and assign attributes and characteristics which are merely projections (Suler, 2004b).

There may only be the representation of a person through online text, with no physical clues which help to provide a more in-depth image of a person. This opens up the possibility to use the imagination regarding who we are interacting with, and also the potential to behave and respond differently to that which is evident during verbal contact, or when in the physical presence of others. There may be occasions where a client enters immediately into self-expression and a release of emotion. The dynamic of online release of emotion, without holding back, is defined as the 'online disinhibition effect' (Suler, 2004b). By having the ability to use the freedom of not being visible, as would be evident in a face-to-face context, it can enable a person to experience liberation in self-expression. This is due to having a sense of not being responsible, or even accountable, for expression.

Suler (2004b) identifies this as 'dissociative anonymity'. The sense of entering into disinhibiting expression and persona freedom can induce either a negative or positive release of feeling, emotion, language use, and so on. Amichai-Hamburger (2005) equates such a release of uninhibited material as an 'iceberg' analogy. Whilst offering the potential for achieving a greater level of insight to conscious and unconscious feelings, it is beneficial for the recipient of disinhibited communication to be mindful of the possibility that the sender may be a novice in online communication and feel uncomfortable at a later point. This may be caused by feeling that they have revealed something about themselves which they had not anticipated and later might regret. Where a positive and supportive online relationship has developed, there is increased potential for such instances to be discussed and not experienced as detrimental either to the ongoing relationship or to the client. An example of this might be where a client who presents for online support has chosen the medium as a route to exploring an issue which feels too uncomfortable to present in a face-to-face context. There may be instances where clients 'test the water' by accessing online support in the context of it feeling a safer place to try to explore an issue which they had not previously discussed with anyone.

Practitioners should be mindful that there may be instances where clients' online disinhibition can be manipulative and unhelpful to supportive interactions. This is apparent where computer-mediated support serves to compound or encourage an 'acting out' of personal issues which would be more appropriately supported within face-to-face interactions. Suler (2004b) defines this as 'toxic disinhibition'.

In a more general context, online support can be viewed as preferable by some clients as they believe their familiarity with the medium allows their feeling expression to be conveyed in a natural manner, similar to that which is experienced in a face-to-face context. For others, where being self-conscious or having low self-esteem has been a factor in seeking online support, this may accentuate the potential for online disinhibition.

The use of acronyms and emoticons

Acronyms

In the context of CMC, acronym is the term for the abbreviation of words which represent an expression of feeling and physical response within asychronous and synchronous interactions. The use of acronyms (Acronyms Online, 2004) can provide a sense of spontaneity and physical expression which takes longer to express in full written form. Using acronyms can therefore be of benefit where an immediate reaction or response is needed. In a group context, where online interaction can move at a quick pace, using acronyms in moderation can allow a person to interact in the flow of a conversation, before the moment in which the feeling is experienced, is lost, and the subject has moved on.

Examples of acronyms are where a response is given in the form of LOL (laughing out loud) or ROFL (rolling on floor laughing). Often these will be emphasised with the use of exclamation marks or inverted commas (LOL !!) or highlighted even further by placing the acronym in bold text. With the absence of visual cues, these can be useful forms of expression and beneficial to the recipient as it provides a more in-depth illustration of the physical and emotional response of the person. It can also bring a sense of personal spontaneity to the dialogue. Excessive use of acronyms could be experienced as an irritation or create a sense of the person being lazy, not fully committed, or engaged in a conversation. In a professional context, this could provide a deeper level of insight to the mood or personality of the individual who expresses themselves in this way.

Emoticons

Emoticons have developed as a greeting using a paralanguage which is widely used in communication contexts such as instant messaging, email, and Internet forums and so on. Online communication using a written format, as opposed to verbal communication, can take longer to convey the 'conversation content', feelings being experienced, or body language. The aptitude of talking is usually achieved more speedily than constructing sentences in the written word. Therefore, the use of emoticons in an online context can serve the purpose of abbreviating what would be present in the written form whilst also giving an instant symbol to others regarding feeling expression, body language, or reactions to what has been stated.

An example of a non-commercially generated emoticon is ☺, which can be formed by using keyboard characters in that order and without spaces. As you can see from Box 3.5, it gives an immediate indication of how someone is feeling without having to use words to describe this. A client's smile might be more pronounced in a physical context than when demonstrated through the use of an emoticon: by using individual preference of colour, font or adopting capitalisation of letters, this may increase the emphasis and personal experience of the sender. The use of imagery can provide a more individual and pronounced tool for conveying online feeling expression, whilst also promoting a deeper level of exploration of the full 'experiencing' of online expression.

Wolf (2000) indicates that women are more likely to find a voice in CMC and adopt the use of emoticons to communicate in non-traditional ways to those which would be evident in face-to-face exchanges. This research also suggests that there may be evidence of gender-swapping in the traditional forms of emotional expression through the use of emoticons. If this is evident within an online supportive environment, it opens up the possibility for men and women to encounter previously uncharted areas of feeling expression. This could prove to be beneficial in assisting both genders in gaining an extended sense of themselves, whilst also discovering new ways of expressing feelings which may be considered less acceptable in a face-to-face context. Wolf identifies that this is apparent within online newsgroups and Huffaker and Calvert (2004) indicates that males average more emoticons in blog postings than females, therefore indicating that online disinhibition may induce greater emotional expression by males than females online which is not usually apparent in the same manner within face-to-face encounters (available at http:// www.davehuffaker.com/papers/davidhuffaker.pdf.).

Client familiarity with acronyms and emoticons

Often clients are fully familiar with online expression and naturally converse using what can be considered as extended online vocabulary, including emoticons and acronyms. Suler (1999) amplifies this by indicating that the lack of face-to-face cues in online interactions has introduced a sophisticated art form of interpersonal expression. Other online clients may have little knowledge or practice in the use of acronyms and emoticons, or may prefer not to use them to highlight emotional and physical response. The online practitioner will need to work in harmony with a client and therefore consideration will need to be given to the appropriate use of tonal and expressive indicators when interacting synchronously or asynchronously.

Summary

The online practitioner will encounter many variations in feeling expression from their clients. This factor will be influenced by the emotional vocabulary available to individual clients, in conjunction with their ability and willingness to express feelings within an online setting. There is a likelihood of some feelings being held at an unconscious level. The skill of the online practitioner is to assist the client in accessing such feelings and enabling expression that supports the positive resolution of personal difficulties and needs which are presented within the online interaction or relationship. With the influence of online disinhibition, there is an increased likelihood that clients may experience a disposition towards conveying enhanced feeling expression during online interaction, in conjunction with disclosing aspects of themselves, their life history, and personal experiences which may not be so evident in face-to-face interactions.

Where this occurs, the online practitioner should be mindful of being sensitive to such disclosures and consider how they would assist a client with the impact this may have and the subsequent support which may be required to prevent a sense of vulnerability within the client. There may be occasions where clients are familiar with a variety of forums for online interaction, some of which may allow a different level of feeling or narrative expression to that which is appropriate to the context of the support provided by online practitioners, and as such adopt a style of feeling expression which is considered inappropriate or offensive to the practitioner. This would be a boundary issue to discuss with a client, as would occur in a face-to-face context.

The acknowledgement and affirmation of online feeling expression is key to a client feeling heard and empathically understood by a practitioner, whilst also providing a basis for further exploration and personal insight for a client. Such recognition by a practitioner will also serve to heighten the engagement with a client and subsequently the quality of the online interaction and relationship.

There will be occasions where a client has specifically selected online support, as opposed to face-to-face assistance due to personal factors and practical considerations, including their familiarity with the medium and experience in conveying feeling expression. There are considerable benefits in having the availability of online support based upon the aforementioned reasons, but there may also be occasions where a person seeks online support due to feeling unable to engage with a practitioner or others in a face-to-face context. If this seems apparent with specific client work, and online support appears to be reinforcing the inability for a client to interact and be expressive in a face-to-face context, the online practitioner will need to reflect upon the relevance of encouraging the individual to consider the potential benefits of engaging with face-to-face support.

With the continuing increase in general awareness and familiarity with the Internet, the potential client base for online support will diversify and increase. As a result of this, there will be a broad range of skills levels and diversity in online feeling expression apparent with clients who present to the practitioner for online support. Not all clients will be familiar with the use of emoticons and acronyms and may feel intimidated or confused by a practitioner who adopts them in an attempt to engage clients. Practitioners may wish to provide information to clients regarding their use, or discuss this as it becomes apparent within online support sessions.

It cannot be assumed that where a client is not able to engage with feeling expression in an online context that the same would apply within face-to-face situations. It may be appropriate to discuss with a client if a face-to-face supportive interaction may be more suited to their needs and assist with a referral if required.

Points for consideration

- What cultural and gender differences may affect a client's ability to express an open account of feeling in an online helping situation, and how might you approach this within your work?
- How might variations in theoretical orientation and helping roles influence the response to a client's expression of feeling when working online?
- How familiar and comfortable are you with the use of online expression such as emoticons or acronyms? How might this benefit or disadvantage your online interaction with clients?
- What are your thoughts regarding online disinhibition and how might you support clients where this becomes evident in a piece of client work?
- What specific groups of potential clients might be advantaged in having the opportunity to engage in the use of online acronym and emoticon expression as a more accessible resource than that which is available to them as clients in face-to-face interactions?

References

Acronyms Online (2004) Available at http://acronymsonline.com/lists/chat_acronyms.asp.

Amichai-Hamburger, Y. (ed.) (2005) *The Social Net: Human Behavior in Cyberspace*. New York: Oxford University Press.

Collie, K., Mitchell, D. and Murphy, L. (2001) 'E-Mail counselling: skills for maximum impact', *Eric/CASS Digest*. p. 2. Available at www.ericdigests.org/2002-3/e-mail.htm.

Feng, J., Lazar, J. and Preece, J. (2003) *Interpersonal Trust and Empathy Online: A Fragile Relationship*. Available at www.ifsm.umbc.edu/~preece/Papers/trust_short_paper_Chi03.pdf.

Huffaker, D.A. and Calvert, S.L. (2005) 'Gender, identity, and language use in teenage blog', *Journal of Computer-Mediated Communication*, 10 (2): article 1. Available at http://jcmc.indiana.edu/vol10/issue2/huffaker.html

Kraus, R., Zack, J. and Stricker, G. (2004) *Online Counselling: A Handbook for Mental Health Professionals*. London: Elsevier. p. 30.

KyungHee, K. and Haejin, Y. (2007) 'Cying for me: cying for us: relational dialetics in a Korean social network site', *Journal of Computer Mediated Communication*, 13 (1). Available at www.blackwell-synergy.com/loi/jcmc?cookieSet=1 and http://jcmc.indiana.edu/vol13/issue1/kim.yun.html.

Manney, P.J. (2006) *Empathy in the Time of Technology: How Storytelling is the Key to Empathy*. Available at www.pj-manney.com/empathy.html.

Preece, J. (1998) 'Empathic communities: reaching out across the Web', *ACM Online Journals*, 5 (2): 32–43. Available at http://doi.acm.org/10.1145/274430.274435.

Stokoe, W. (2001) Language in Hand: Why Sign Came Before Speech. Washington, DC: Gaulledet University Press. p. 62.

Suler, J. (1999) *E-Mail Communication and Relationships*. Available at www.rider.edu/~suler/psycyber/index.html.

Suler, J. (2003) *The Psychology of Cyberspace: E-mail Communication and Relationships*. Available at www-usr.rider.edu/~suler/psycyber/emailrel.html.

Suler, J. (2004a) *Psychotherapy in Cyberspace: A Model of Pychotherapy in Cyberspace*. Available at http://users.rider.edu/~suler/psycyber/therapy.html.

Suler, J. (2004b) *The Online Disinhibition Effect*. Available at www-usr.rider.edu/~suler/psycyber/disinhibit.html.

Tolan, J. (2003) *Skills in Person-centred Counselling and Psychotherapy*. London: Sage. p. 151.

Wolf, A. (2000) *CyberPsychology and Behavior*, 3 (5): 827–33. Available at www.liebert online.com/doi/abs/10.1089/10949310050191809.

Zelvin, E. (2003) 'Treating addictions in cyberspace', *Journal of Social Work Practice in the Addictions*, 3 (3): 105–112.

Further reading, references, resources, and skill development activities relating to the subject matter within this chapter can be sourced via the companion website to this book.

ONLINE LISTENING, ATTUNEMENT AND ATTENDING TO THE CLIENT

Online counselling skills presented in this chapter:

- Communicating your presence, interest, and attention when 'listening' online
- Developing and maintaining attunement with a client

Exercises and vignettes are included within this chapter, demonstrating the skills in practice and encouraging thought on the subject matter discussed.

This chapter discusses the skills of listening, attending, and forming attunement with clients. Such aptitudes are essential features of an effective online practice. The absence of a client's physical presence within computer-mediated interaction requires a more focused and creative approach by the practitioner during the process of developing attunement and understanding of the client and their presenting issues. It is also the responsibility of the online practitioner to facilitate an online exchange where both parties can be 'heard' and enabled in listening to the other person (Kraus et al., 2004).

The skills discussed in this chapter contribute to the overall sense of clients experiencing a sense of the practitioner being actively engaged, attentive, and 'listening' during online exchanges. As within face-to-face exchanges, it is important for practitioners to identify any evident blocks which restrict their full attention during the process of listening to and attuning with a client, as otherwise this may restrict the potential to develop sufficient rapport (Nelson-Jones, 2005).

Communicating your presence, interest, and attention when 'listening' online

This subject area covers two categories:

- communicating an online presence, interest, and attention in a general context of engaging with clients; and
- communicating your presence whilst 'listening' to client narrative.

Communicating an online presence in a general context of supporting clients

Each human being emanates a presence, whether in a face-to-face or online context. It is a dynamic which forms a part of the process of defining who we are as individuals, and how we are experienced by others. When meeting people within a face-to-face interaction, a person's presence will be evident in a physical context and this contributes to many features in how others would describe what that presence represents. When interacting online, with the absence of physical and auditory representations, there is still the opportunity for an individual sense of presence and a therapeutic alliance to be formed and experienced by both client and practitioner.

Research indicates that such an experiencing of presence is significant within video-conferencing media (Wootton et al., 2003). The personality attributes of an individual will still be evident during computer-mediated communication (CMC), albeit in a different form to that which is available during face-to-face interactions. The primary function of an online supportive interaction is to provide professional assistance to clients, whilst also seeking to establish a relationship, whether this is formed during a single interaction or developed over a number of sessions. The online practitioner will be seeking to establish themselves with clients and included within this process will be aspects of their personality being conveyed during the delivery of their service. As such, presence forms an important feature within online supportive relationships due to the unavailability of physical and auditory attributes. Clients still require a strong sense of a practitioner's presence and their ability to be attentive and responsive to their needs. It is the content and structure of the practitioner's narrative and the professionalism in which they deliver their service that is experienced by a client. This forms a key aspect of experiencing a practitioner's presence. Being mindful of this throughout the process of engaging with a client and developing the online relationship is integral to professional practice and the resulting quality of service a client experiences.

Communicating your presence whilst 'listening' to client narrative

This second feature, of practitioners communicating their presence whilst listening to a client, refers to how listening is explicitly demonstrated as a client is presenting narrative during computer-mediated exchanges. During face-to-face interchanges, a practitioner can provide clear indications that they are listening to a client by the use of eye contact, body language, and auditory indications. A client has the reassurance of knowing that the practitioner is still in the room with them due to being present in a physical context. Within an online context, a practitioner has to adopt other indicators to inform clients that they are listening and being attentive.

During computer-mediated interactions, both parties are reliant on technology to keep them together in the 'online practitioner's room', which at times can be affected by technology issues or disruption to Internet connections and so on. With this potential risk of breakdown in communication, either client or practitioner can be left requiring reassurance that the other party is still available and able to resume communication. When a client is communicating online narrative, particularly if it extends over a period of a few minutes, it is important that they are given reassurances by the practitioner that they are still present and 'listening' to the client. This may be discussed at the onset of engaging with clients by practitioners highlighting how they will signify their consistent listening during times when clients are providing information or conveying more than a paragraph or so of narrative.

The importance of communicating presence is particularly pertinent during an initial online meeting as clients may present large amounts of information to the practitioner. A client's general level of anxiety could be heightened if they are concerned by an absence of listening reassurances being conveyed by the practitioner during their presentation of information or narrative.

Examples of a practitioner demonstrating their presence whilst listening to their client can be any of the following, in addition to personalised styles of conveying presence whilst listening:

- A series of full stops at appropriate intervals between client narrative, which will appear as:
  Jane says: ....
- The written form of 'Hmm…..' or other signifier of listening to replace the verbal equivalent which would be apparent in a face-to-face interaction.
- Narratively expressing the words 'I'm still here', or 'I'm listening'.

Developing and maintaining attunement with a client

When listening to another person in a face-to-face setting, a practitioner pays attention to the verbal dialogue of a client, whilst taking note of other characteristics within the presentation of the content. There will also be evidence of non-verbal indicators, which may promote a more in-depth understanding of the individual and the issues being presented, whilst also reinforcing a client's ability to strengthen their sense of self (Greenberg et al., 1993; Magnavita, 2004).

Imagine yourself sitting with a client at this moment in time and consider how you would attempt to gain the maximum in listening to their dialogue and forming an understanding in order to begin the process of providing support. You would be noting the following, in conjunction with observing the client's overall presentation:

- verbal content
- pitch of voice
- fluidity of speech and pauses or gaps in between subject matter or feeling expression
- pacing of verbal dialogue
- level of eye contact offered whilst talking, as well as subject and feeling expression areas where eye contact is avoided
- apparent silences or areas where the client appears to block themselves from entering into discussion on difficult subject areas
- body language
- visual and verbal characteristics of the person, including gender, cultural origin, disability, and personal faith.

There may be a tendency to take some of these features of being an attentive listener for granted when working in a face-to-face context, but remain integral to the overall skill of taking note of the comprehensive indications present when in a face-to-face interaction with clients. Some of these skills cannot translate into online working for obvious reasons, nonetheless it is possible to 'fine tune' those skills which are adaptable into online work. As skilled listeners, we have more than auditory senses to utilise when 'listening' to a client.

The following section includes the skills previously listed which have been adapted to illustrate those which can be used by the professional when conducting online CMC.

Verbal content

Verbal content becomes the presented 'written narrative'. Although practitioners will not hear the client's voice unless both parties are using an online microphone system, there is the opportunity to read and 'hear' the verbal content through the conveyed written narrative generated in online exchanges.

Using the examples in Box 4.1 and Box 4.2, we can consider how the written narrative is being conveyed and how it might differ if presented in a verbal account. The examples include both asynchronous and synchronous contexts, thereby demonstrating how differences in the medium may influence the transference of verbal communication into a written narrative or structure.

An example is provided from an initial simulated email from a client.

Box 4.1   Verbal content as written narrative

Hey ....

I feel I have a lot to say in my email, so if the content is too long please let me know and I'll make it shorter next time.

I'm finding it difficult to manage my financial situation at the moment as I have got myself into debt due to credit cards and a loan for a new car. It's starting to affect my health as I'm constantly worrying about how I'll pay the bills each month. I haven't been able to talk to my partner about this as she's really careful with money and always plans ahead. She would never use credit cards or take out loans either, so she wouldn't understand and it would only make the stress of the situation worse. I've always had a problem with managing money, but recently it's feeling out of control. I need some support with deciding how I can change the situation I'm in. It can't carry on like this or I will lose my home and my partner ....

In the example provided within Box 4.1, the content is direct and precise. The opening greeting sounds quite informal and relaxed, but the general tone within the email expresses a sense of urgency to deal with the problem due to financial and personal implications for the client if continuing with the current level of debt. The subject content and description of the presenting issues can also appear briefer than if presented by spoken word as sentences can be shortened and elaborations such as those used in a face-to-face context are often not included. There appears to be a sense of urgency to resolve their difficulties, whilst also wanting to 'spill out' all of the problems that have been a concern in the time leading up to seeking support. This may place the practitioner under pressure to offer a quick and directive response. This point is highlighted further by each sentence holding a new aspect to the overall theme of support required.

For those professionals who support clients in a face-to-face context, this may feel similar to meeting a client on the first occasion who brings a list of things they would want to discuss and presents the contents as a direct feature of importance to the meeting. During a first online or face-to-face meeting, a practitioner can feel as though they have been left with a lot to 'hold' or respond to.

Receiving an asynchronous request from a client with content such as that contained within Box 4.1 could leave the recipient feeling a sense of urgency and responsibility to offer solutions, where the preferred response would contain encouragement to the client in being proactive in exploring the possible options in alleviating the difficulty of their circumstances. This feature of assisting a client in problem solving is discussed in detail in Chapter 2.

If the same content was presented within a face-to-face context, there may be further indications for the receiver of the dialogue in how urgent the situation was, perhaps denoted by tone of voice, body language and so on. In an email reply to the client (Box 4.1), it is important to convey an understanding of the written narrative and encourage the client to provide a more in-depth account of the concerns they had expressed in their first communication with the practitioner. During initial exchanges, a client may be hesitant in offering too much in written form whilst they are consciously or unconsciously trying to gain a sense of who they are interacting with, in conjunction with determining the level of confidence they can place in the practitioner. During CMC, there may be instances where clients are less anxious and inhibited regarding 'spilling out' their presenting difficulties than would be apparent during face-to-face encounters. The anonymity of online communication can reduce the likelihood of feelings relating to embarrassment, guilt, and shame. There is also the likelihood that a client constructing a written narrative is less likely to present contradictions than in verbal communication (Murphy and Mitchell, 1998).

Box 4.2 is an example provided from an initial simulated synchronous chat dialogue, where John is the client and Pete is the service practitioner. The meeting has been pre-arranged and John has arrived a little late for the 'session'. It is also John's first experience of seeking synchronous support online with an online counsellor.

Box 4.2   Initial email exchanges

Pete: Hi john..... I was waiting for you to appear online....i thought you may have had problems with your internet connection. How are you... are you okay to begin our session this evening?

(Continued)

(Continued)

John: Hi Pete, good thanks arrived home late from work. This is the first time I've ever used this so I may be a little slow, apologies

Pete: don't worry we have an hour for our meeting and I can offer support if you are unsure of anything………

John: Great! Now how does it work? Do you ask questions and I answer them?

Pete: i'll ask a few questions along the way…. and give you space to think and so on and talk where you need to...

[Pause]

Pete: it's your 'session' so I'll let you lead it as it feels best for you……..do you have any initial questions before we begin

John: OK. No questions it was all clear in your initial email which I received. The booklet on how to use the service, confidentiality etc was also helpful.

Pete: Good…..I'm glad you feel the booklet was helpful. Perhaps you could begin by telling me some background to the issue you would like to explore in our meetings together?

John: OK. I'd like to understand why I suffer with bouts of depression that have been ongoing over the last 4 or 5 years. It affects my work and friendships/relationships. I often distance myself from people when I'm feeling depressed and this then makes matters worse.

In Box 4.2, the initial content of the meeting involves a discussion regarding John's late arrival for the session and a brief clarification of how to conduct the session. In this example, some time has been lost in providing an explanation and 'settling in' to the first meeting, prior to focusing on the presenting issues. When using synchronous computer-mediated technology, it is beneficial to have included some prior asynchronous contact as proportionately the written narrative which is available through synchronous working can be considerably less. When a client has sent an initial outline of the presenting difficulties to the practitioner prior to the meeting, in conjunction with a practitioner providing guidelines on working synchronously, this reduces the time taken up with contracting and other preliminary issues during the first synchronous appointment.

In the example provided, John appears to be able to express his thoughts and concerns clearly in written format. Synchronous exchanges may provide more evident insight to this than other CMC, as both client and practitioner do not have the same access to spell-check or the same level of time to construct a reply.

The initial impression of John during this first interaction indicates a sense of self-confidence and preciseness in how he responds to the practitioner. He feels confident enough to ask for clarification, where unsure of how to proceed, and is courteous in offering information as to his late arrival for the session. His use of exclamation marks and abbreviation of words like 'okay' indicate directness and an ability to be assertive when needed. The overall sense of John's written narrative illustrates confidence in self-expression and the articulation of words and the aptitude to translate this into CMC.

EXERCISE 4.1

NARRATIVE CONTENT IN EMAILS

What additional features of narrative content are apparent to you in Boxes 4.1 and 4.2, and how might your replies differ or be further developed to those provided by the simulated practitioner response?

Pitch of voice

Pitch of voice can be experienced in an online context as a feature of a client presenting written words in different font or colours, highlighting words in bold, using exclamation marks and question marks, or capitalising words and letters. A further example of pitch variation can be demonstrated by **BYE!! for now** .... or **HELLO!!**ooooooo...... You will have noted that as the extended word moves from capitals, bold text and exclamation marks to lower case letters, it provides a sense of how the word is being spoken and the pitch used in an online context. The use of full stops at the end can also signify a sense of the other's online 'voice' becoming fainter, ending in an extended form to emphasise the depth of feeling, or convey a greater awareness of something mentioned in a dilaogue. Words can be adapted in this manner to illustrate a written pitch, depth, or quality, and provide an indication of what the sender is trying to convey, either consciously or unconsciously.

Box 4.3 provides an example which includes elements of pitch of voice in a simulated email from an ongoing client, where a strong therapeutic alliance has developed over a number of email exchanges.

Box 4.3 Pitch of voice conveyed in an email

Hi Petra,

It has been sooooo....hard for me to write this email. I feel that the situation with my boss has become much more difficult recently as she does not take on board my feelings regarding the pressure I'm under at work. I decided that if I could just say how I felt here it might help to clear my head and then allow me to think about it more calmly and find a way of handling it better. So here goes!!!

My boss is NOT an EXPERT on everything at work!!! She is NOT PERFECT! She takes her own frustration out on everyone else, and doesn't really seem to give a thought or care about it. SHE IS NEVER RESPONSIBLE FOR HER MISTAKES! Someone else is always responsible. Yet, she does make mistakes a lot and blames others for the outcome. SHE IS SO UNFAIR in how she treats the people who work with her, PARTICULARLY ME!! She has such a distorted view of things that it irritates the .... out of me! It leaves me feeling UNDERVALUED and de-motivated most of the time. I wish she would leave and then I could concentrate on my work and being happy!!!!!! I wish she was here now so that I could say these things to her, and that she would LISTEN to me.

The client's use of capitalisation and exclamation marks in Box 4.3 provides an illustration of the emphasis of feelings, whilst also indicating that if the narrative was presented in a verbal dialogue, the pitch of voice and the feeling expression would be heightened and more profound when expressing particular aspects of the content. This offers the practitioner a more insightful understanding of how the client is experiencing her feelings towards the work situation and her boss. This in turn paves the way for constructing a reply to the client where a deeper level of empathic response can be conveyed. The client is also indicating that expressing certain written narrative in this manner will allow her to begin to reflect in a calmer manner, therefore allowing herself to express her anger and settle into a place where she could consider things in a more calm and insightful manner.

In the example provided in Box 4.3, the pitch of the narrative could have been heightened further if the simulated client had highlighted the capitalised words with bold or a particular colour to increase the impact of the text.

Instances where pitch of voice or feeling expression is not apparent Box 4.3 provides an illustration of this where a client is openly expressing their feelings or using identifying aspects relating to pitch of voice and providing the practitioner with a strong sense of the feeling range experienced whilst writing the text. It cannot be assumed that where a client does not explicitly express feelings, either in synchronous or asynchronous communication, that they are not being experienced by the client. It could be that the client is fully engaged with their feelings when discussing issues and recollections they have brought to the online session, but are not disclosing them due to any or all of the following reasons:

- feelings arise unexpectedly
- embarrassment or discomfort when revealing feelings
- uncertainty in how the practitioner will respond
- not wishing to appear vulnerable.

When interacting with and supporting clients in a face-to-face context or via telephone contact, the practitioner will have access to auditory, visual, and physical cues to indicate that the client is experiencing feelings or a level of distress. When working online, such cues may be absent and therefore it is vital not to make assumptions that an absence of written narrative indicates the client is not experiencing a range of feelings.

In face-to-face therapeutic work, there are instances of clients making a 'door handle' statement which can prove to be revealing of feelings or something which they had not disclosed in the session. Similar occurrences may arise during computer-mediated exchanges, and as a result can leave both practitioner and client feeling that the meeting had ended in a manner which was not beneficial to either party. This can be particularly evident where the client has not explicitly expressed their feelings in the course of a session, but has chosen to leave it to the end of a meeting to reveal that they had been emotionally impacted by an aspect of the interaction or memories which had arisen. It is therefore always advisable for the practitioner to remain 'tuned' to the client's words throughout the content of both a synchronous and asynchronous dialogue exchange.

It is beneficial to leave an adequate amount of time at the end of synchronous exchanges to provide an opportunity for the practitioner to close the session, whilst also checking if any issues had arisen that the client would wish to make the practitioner aware of. By having this awareness, the practitioner can make preparation for 'tuning' in to the client's dialogue in a different manner during a subsequent session in order to pick up any non-evident explicit cues where feelings or distress are being experienced by a client. Where instances such as this have occurred, it is also beneficial to spend some time at the beginning of the following session encouraging the client to discuss what they need from the practitioner to assist with managing and expressing feelings as they arise.

🄴🄓🄴🄡🄒🄘🄢🄴   🄸.🄸

PITCH OF VOICE

Upon reflection of the examples provided in Box 4.3, consider how you might interpret or express the pitch of voice in an online context with the following list of emotions:

- excitement
- happiness
- fear
- anxiety
- sadness
- low mood
- frustration
- anger.

If you are able to, share your thoughts with a colleague. Compare and discuss similarities or differences in how you have expressed pitch within the context of these feelings.

Fluidity of speech and pauses or gaps in between subject matter or feeling expression

When interacting in a face-to-face situation, we are present in a physical context to note where gaps in the other's speech occurs, and often gain a sense of why this may have occurred. When working in the context of asynchronous exchanges, the writer may punctuate a break or ending in the flow of a subject area by beginning a new paragraph, and may even leave the previous subject manner incomplete, or with an abrupt ending. This may provide an indication of where it has been difficult to continue or complete an area of thought or discussion, which could relate to the level of feeling disturbance the client is experiencing whilst communicating. This may also indicate that a client has a learning difficulty or mental health issue which affects the flow of their thought processes.

You may have noted from the examples of simulated client work illustrated throughout this book that during synchronous computer-mediated communication, I have used a short sequence of full stops at the end of a line to indicate where either the practitioner or client intends to continue with a thread of discussion. An example of this can be found in Box 4.2:

Pete:

don't worry we have an hour for our meeting and I can offer support if you are unsure of anything.........

The full stops signify that Pete has not finished a thread of discussion, but has 'released' a piece of text onto the shared screen so that the recipient is not left for a lengthy period of time waiting for text to appear on the shared dialogue screen. This practice assists with the flow of conversation and prevents the other party being distracted whilst following and participating in the dialogue.

Using this 'signal' of continuing dialogue also prevents conversations overlapping or subject matter changing before the thread of discussion has ended. Where a group of people are interacting, this is particularly useful as an indicator for others to wait for completion of one person's input prior to others offering a reply or moving on to another subject discussion area.

You may also have noted that there are occasions where a sequence of full stops is used to signify pauses in thought or a change in the flow of content during one line of text, as in Box 4.2:

Pete:

It's your 'session' so I'll let you lead it as it feels best for you.........do you have any initial questions before we begin

This style can be useful in both asynchronous and synchronous CMC as a visual indication of natural pauses which occur in verbal sentence structure and change in subject matter.

EXERCISE 4.3

FLUIDITY OF SPEECH

Consider what additional methods of highlighting dialogue continuation or natural flow of narrative presentation can be adopted within both asynchronous and synchronous exchanges. Sharing this activity with a colleague could provide valuable feedback on how this might be experienced when using it within client work.

Pacing of verbal dialogue

When communicating online, in either a synchronous or asynchronous context, without the facility of a medium that provides voice call (which is available with software such as Skype or MSN Messenger), this aspect of face-to-face working can translate across to a heading defined as 'pacing of narrative'. The pacing of verbal dialogue does hold some similarities to those discussed in the section on verbal content, and further endorses the similarities which would be evident in comparing these facets of face-to-face interaction.

I will outline how this may convert to both synchronous and asynchronous computer-mediated communication without actual voice content using examples which hold differing dynamics behind the nature of how the pacing of narrative is evident. Within professional online practice, there may be many more variations which are evident within a client's pacing of both synchronous and asynchronous communication. I have provided two examples as a basis for illustrating this feature of online communication and leave you, the practitioner, to consider further variations and their relevance as they arise within your professional practice.

Asynchronous communication   Within face-to-face communication, a client may talk in a rapid pace where sentences flow from one straight into another without a reasonable pause to allow the listener to take in information during the flow of dialogue. If this is translated across to written narrative, there are similarities as the text appears as a piece of unpunctuated communication where the subjects matter changes without pause or space or time for reflection by the writer. When this occurs within a face-to-face context, the listener may feel confused and even overwhelmed by the volume and content of the exchange. This usually represents a level of urgency or anxiety being experienced by the presenter of the communication, as they rush to convey the details relating to the subject. Often in face-to-face encounters, the pace of the verbal presentation is influenced by the conscious and unconscious emotions associated with the content of the material being verbally expressed, and the extent of content which the client wishes to convey.

There may be occasions where a person does not consider the word count guidelines which have been suggested prior to commencing ongoing support. This may result in the narrative pacing being rapid and extending the asynchronous dialogue to a word count beyond the time in which the recipient of the material can read and form a reply within a single exchange. A client will often realise after writing their email that they have included too much narrative and ask the practitioner to clarify this in their reply.

Some clients experience the task of constructing their email as difficult for a variety of reasons and the resulting pacing of narrative is slow, which is reflected in the minimal level of content received by the practitioner.

Box 4.4   Pacing of an asynchronous dialogue

I'm sending through my weekly email to you with a few thoughts and questions regarding my progress with self-help sheets you sent last time

I tried to complete the sheet which asked questions about how I'd felt over the last week but I find it hard to get time to sit down in the evenings and think about what's happened in my day and write it all down. You mentioned last

> time that I would need to put time aside for it but it's not easy for me to do that with everything else that's happening at home with family life. i'll try it again this week and see how I get on. Work is really busy at the moment and I feel tired in the evening too. The relaxation sheet you gave me was helpful and I managed to find time last night to try it out. I did feel okay afterwards (more relaxed than usual). John, my partner took the children out for a walk so that helped too. In respect of my eating patterns I've talked with my Gp and he's offered to refer me to a dietician at the hospital, just have to wait for an appointment......

Box 4.4 provides an example of where the pacing of narrative is hasty and flows quickly from one point of discussion to another without a pause or extended reflection on the topic presented. The client has sent the email without spell-checking it first, resulting in errors. The absence of an opening greeting to the practitioner indicates a detachment from the person who will be receiving the email. This may be a feature of how the client communicates asynchronously, or represents a further aspect of the hurried nature in how the email was written. The overall structure and content of this email may well represent a similarity to how the client is experiencing a lack of order and suitable time management in their personal life, and therefore offers insight which can be considered in the practitioner's reply.

Synchronous communication When working synchronously with clients, the pacing of narrative is clearly more apparent as both parties are communicating in real time, therefore making the pacing visible as it occurs during the flow of communication. Within this CMC, there is a natural opportunity for the practitioner to observe and explore with a client any apparent fluctuations in the pacing of the written narrative.

In Box 4.5, Julie has suggested a synchronous meeting with Sam as their asynchronous exchanges do not appear to be generating a sense of connection and forming of the required online relationship. Julie felt it may be the choice of asynchronous contact which was impacting upon this. They agree to meet for one session to try to enhance the online rapport and attunement.

Box 4.5 Synchronous dialogue via email

Julie: Hello Sam. How have you been this last week?

Sam: Hi ....it's been okay

Julie: As I had mentioned in my email, I felt meeting synchronously today might be beneficial to us both in getting to a point where you feel that

(Continued)

(Continued)

> your concerns regarding your daughter are moving to a more positive place, and also I was a little uncertain if email support was proving to distance you from me as your counsellor
>
> *Sam*:   Okay.....It does feel better talking in this way with you
> *Julie*: Shall we spend a few minutes at the end of the meeting deciding how to move forward with appointments
> *Sam*:   okay that would be good
> *Julie*: Was there something in particular that you wanted to talk about today?
>
> [There is a few moments pause before Julie can see Sam writing a response. She consciously holds back for her to reply. If the delay had lasted longer she might have asked Sam if she was OK, whilst also ascertaining if she was pausing before considering her reply.]
>
> *Sam*:   I had another fall out with my daughter this week
> *Julie*: Would you like to talk about that as it feels as though it was something that stands out above anything else?
>
> [Again there is a lengthy pause before Sam begins to type a response and Julie waits rather than interrupting.]
>
> *Sam*:   Okay. Don't really know where to start though......

In Box 4.5, aspects of the client's narrative pace are very slow, particularly when considering how to discuss issues which have occurred during the last week. The practitioner is immediately aware of this and consciously decides to wait before remarking on it to the client. The decision is based upon Sam being a relatively new client and Julie not yet being familiar enough with Sam's synchronous writing style to know if this is her usual pace, or whether there are other factors involved. If the narrative pace continued in this manner, Julie may ask Sam if she is experiencing any personal difficulties or emotional responses which were affecting her ability to reply without a considerable delay.

EXERCISE   4.4

PACING

How might you approach the subject of pacing with clients within synchronous exchanges? What considerations would influence how you might approach this subject with clients?

Level of eye contact offered whilst talking, as well as subject and feeling expression areas where eye contact is avoided

This feature of listening and attending skills is not transferable to CMC unless utilising a webcam for synchronous meetings with clients. When using a webcam or other aid where the person is visible, paying attention to eye contact will be more restricted than in face-to-face contact. This is due to the requirement to be involved in other activities, such as typing during the course of the online exchange. Nonetheless, this does provide some advantage over a complete absence of visual indicators.

Subject and feeling expression areas where eye contact is avoided   With the absence of a physical presence during online counselling exchanges, there will not be the same opportunity to notice where a client avoids direct contact when speaking. In face-to-face contexts, this can represent a client experiencing a feeling of embarrassment, shame, or anticipation that they may be judged by the practitioner, and so avoid being in receipt of disapproval or judgement by averting their eyes from direct contact with the other person. There may also be occasions where a client looks away from the practitioner whilst considering how to form a reply or structure the content of a piece of communication. In such instances, this may not be related to feelings which are described in the former example of eye contact avoidance or aversion.

When interacting with clients using asynchronous dialogues, such as email exchanges, the practitioner would not have an indication of eye contact avoidance unless the client had included information relating to this as a reflection within the content of their communication. When synchronously engaging with a client, such visual eye contact aversions may be apparent due to breaks in the flow of dialogue, or when the practitioner can visually see that the client has begun to construct a sentence but notices a pause in their writing. This can be particularly helpful when using an instant relay chat medium as both practitioner and client will usually have a visual indicator that shows when either party is writing text. This facility can therefore give insight to where a break in eye contact with the computer screen or thought process has occurred, and where it may be appropriate to invite a client to share what may have caused the pause in their writing.

EXERCISE 4.5

DEALING WITH PAUSES

How would you envisage being able to maintain a focus and concentration when there are lengthy pauses due to a client requiring more time to construct their thoughts and form a synchronous reply?

🄴🅇🄴🅁🄲🄸🅂🄴   🄴.🄶

STEERING A CLIENT

Consider how you might encourage a client to identify where uncomfortable thoughts or feelings are causing the client to divert their attention?

Apparent silences or areas where the client appears to block themselves from entering into discussion on difficult subject areas

During online interactions, there is the absence of visual indicators which illustrate apparent silences in the same manner as would occur in a face-to-face exchange. The manner in which it may become evident during a synchronous online interaction is highlighted in the simulated client example provided in Box 4.6, where Mia is a worker employed in a voluntary online agency providing synchronous online support to young Asian women.

Box 4.6   Dealing with difficult pauses

Mia: Hello Shirin....you mentioned last week that you would like to talk about finding somewhere local to continue your study after finishing sixth-form study...and also the subject you want to study. Would you like to start with that today?

Shirin: Hi Mia. Things have changed since last time and I'm not sure I need to talk about that any more.

Mia: Can you say more about that Shirin as last week you seemed really keen to discuss it?

Shirin: No it's okay I think I just want to talk about something else this time

Mia: Sure that's fine Shirin. If you feel it's already been resolved we can talk about something else.

Shirin: I'm not sure if coming to the agency was a good idea really as it's not helping me to sort things out in the way I'd hoped.

Mia: Can you say more about that Shirin as I'm not clear why you feel that way?

Shirin: Well I talk here... but nothing really changes. I can't really see how it can change

[Mia notices that Shirin began to type something further but then stopped. Mia waits for a moment or two then sends the following question.]

> *Mia*: I noticed you were typing something else Shirin, but I didn't receive any text on the screen... was there something you wanted to say?
>
> [After a moment or so Shirin sends her reply, although it is evident to Mia that she stopped and started typing several times before 'releasing' any text onto the screen.]
>
> *Shirin*: My parents make decisions for me about my study and where to study. So there's no point in me talking about it here as I just feel more upset about not having any choices
>
> [The dialogue continues with Mia asking Shirin if she would like to talk about her frustration with the conflict between her own and her parents' wishes for Shirin's future.]

In Box 4.6, although there was no visual contact between the practitioner and client, Mia has an awareness that her client is feeling reluctant to pursue conversation in a subject area which she had previously identified as a priority. Clearly, there are underlying reasons for the client avoiding discussion on the subject, but with considered encouragement, the practitioner endeavours to support the client in exploring the underlying issue which is not being explicitly expressed. The practitioner has picked up on the 'visual' indications of the client experiencing a block in revealing the issue which is concerning her, and provides a supportive opening for Shirin to look at what might be contributing to her avoidance of the issue.

🄴🄾🄴🅁🄲🄸🅂🄴 🄴.🄴

DEALING WITH PAUSES

Consider how you would encourage and support a client in face-to-face exchanges where apparent 'blocks' occur. How might your skills in this area transfer across to online exchanges?

Body language

Unless the client has supplied a personal photograph, adopts an avatar to illustrate their online persona, or is visible via a webcam, there is an obvious lack of visual presence when working online with clients.

A photograph or avatar is also static and only captures impressions of body language in the context of when a photograph was taken, or at the point the avatar image was adopted. Where a client has provided a photographic image, this can be useful as a tool for gaining insight to characteristics of the person, even if only to the point of being able to see the pose and body mannerisms at the time the photograph was taken. If practitioner and client use webcams during synchronous exchanges, there will be a limited advantage of being able to observe body language as both parties may also be typing and therefore not continuously looking at the other person. When using a microphone for speech communication in conjunction with a webcam, this will move the potential to observe body language to a closer likeness in that of face-to-face communication.

Visual and verbal characteristics of the person, including gender, cultural origin, disability, and personal faith

During computer-mediated exchanges, the verbal characteristics of a client's presentation transfer from a face-to-face context as dialogue expression and narrative connotations. There will be distinct differences in these two features, which are heightened by factors such as gender, cultural origin, disability, and personal faith. Lago and Smith (2003) provide a practitioner guide to promoting awareness and professional development to counteract the potential impact of such features within therapeutic relationships.

There are also the influences of social, economic, and demographic features which will be present. Prior to considering these factors, it is important to take into account that there will be a personal framework in how each client structures and presents the content of their dialogue expression and narrative connotations. These features will vary according to the external and personal influences being experienced by the individual, both in the past, the present, and the future. The manner in which a client presents during computer-mediated exchanges and structures their communication and its content is therefore influenced by many factors, and is multi-layered. Such differences can be experienced as magnified within online interactions, particularly where clients are sourced from countries of origin which are demographically different to the practitioner (Suler and Fenichel, 2000). This occurs in the practitioner's encountering of clients within a face-to-face setting, but has differing nuances within the context of computer-mediated exchanges. It is important to consider and note this to inform the skills of listening, attending, and attunement to a client.

To further qualify the terms of dialogue expression and narrative connotations, the following explanation of the terms may assist in providing clarification:

- *Dialogue expression* The word dialogue represents spoken words, conversation, or literature in the form of a conversation. CMC, although usually in written form, consists of the words and conversation between two or more people. It is in essence the conversation which occurs in CMC. It often includes the presence of internal thought processes, which can be denoted by the visible insertion of words within brackets or the use of other symbols to create awareness for the reader that internal thoughts or feelings are being conveyed and shared. The manner in which a client adopts their dialogue expression will vary, just as it occurs within face-to-face interaction. This is present as a unique personal watermark of each client.

- *Narrative connotations*   Within the context of literature, the word 'narrative' is defined as telling a story, giving an account of something, or recounting the sequence of events that are related to a process or occurrence. If two people were given the task of verbally conveying the same narrative to another person, there would be variations in how they each applied connotations to the presenting of the narrative, which in turn personalise the delivery of it. In addition, this may have the effect of changing the meaning behind the words. This often occurs when particular emphasis is placed on words, or pauses are included where not necessarily indicated within the text. This holds a similar feature within online communication as each client will bring a personalised style of narrative connotation.

A practitioner can use their understanding and familiarity with the individual characteristic of each client's online presentation to gain insight in how best to develop rapport with a client, whilst also noting changes in dialogue expression in conjunction with narrative connotations, and the significance of this.

Varying personal influences on dialogue expression and narrative connotations
To illustrate the variations that may become apparent, take a few moments to consider how you might write an email to a friend with the intention of informing them that you are going away for a few days on a business trip. Next consider how the email content and style may vary if you were writing it in the following circumstances:

1. At the beginning or end of the day.
2. When under pressure to complete another task.
3. When you had just received some bad news.
4. After having a disagreement with someone close to you.
5. When looking forward to the trip in contrast to experiencing a resistance to go.

Although the intention of the email communication remains static, each of the circumstances listed above would influence, to varying degrees, how the dialogue expression and narrative connotations would be presented within the email. All of these variations, alongside more defined gender, cultural, disability, and personal faith differences, will be apparent during online communication. These are considerations which the practitioner will be able to utilise to gain insight into their clients and presenting issues, particularly where an ongoing relationship is formed due to the variations which are influenced by personal and external factors.

The colloquial terms and dialect will be evident and can provide insight into elements of a client's mannerisms and their origin. Within face-to-face communication, you may have two clients who present to a service for support with the same presenting issues yet the manner in which they verbally recount material to a practitioner will be individual and unique. This occurs in the same manner during computer-mediated exchanges. The individual narrative style and the form in how this is presented will vary with each online client and is naturally influenced by many factors beyond the direct differences of gender, cultural origin, disability, and personal faith.

Dialogue expression and narrative connotations relating to gender, disability, cultural, and personal faith features within online communication When supporting others in a face-to-face interaction or relationship, the facets of difference and diversity presented by each client will generally be evident due to there being a physical encounter. This provides a visual perspective that offers a level of insight and awareness which is not readily available when conducting an online practice. The potential to engage with others within a global interface naturally enhances the opportunity for practitioners to encounter clients from a broader range of cultural base, origin, and social and economic context. This requires consideration and awareness by practitioners, as they will not have access to the same opportunities for visual and audio indications to signify a need in accommodating apparent difference in how a client may present their dialogue expression or narrative connotations.

Within face-to-face encounters, a valuable tool to assist in opening and continuing a dialogue, where such diversity occurs, is encouraging discussion on perceptions of difference (Nelson-Jones, 2003). By not addressing such factors, this can adversely impact upon rapport and the relationship (Multi Cultural Issues Board, 1996). The same principles apply when engaged in computer-mediated supportive relationships with clients.

The variations which can occur across a global perspective are too numerous to highlight within this section, but the key considerations for an online practitioner fall into two main areas:

1. The apparent difference in how a client expresses themselves necessitates sensitivity by the practitioner and time for reflection on how the online communication can be facilitated and developed to provide the appropriate environment which is conducive to the interaction and relationship. The responsibility lies with practitioners to establish an interchange where both parties feel 'heard' and understood.
2. In addition to considerations regarding the individual features of a client's dialogue expression and narrative connotations, it is important to reflect on gender, cultural, disability, origin, and personal faith differences. These feature as a further layer of variation in client presentations. There may be

an increased tendency to stereotype and pre-judge clients when encountering difference in an online setting as there is an absence of physical presence and visual indications. There is an increased likelihood to adopt the use of projection or transference responses. If a practitioner forms an image of their online client as a means of consolidating their engagement with the person, this may lead to projections based upon prejudiced and biased perceptions of the client. It is therefore important for online practitioners to note that this may occur, and monitor their image interpretations of clients to avoid such projections which may subsequently impair the client relationship.

Summary

The skills discussed within this chapter form key aspects in the process of communicating, listening, forming a relationship, and attunement with clients. They are the basis of how an online practitioner conveys their understanding of the client and the individual presentation of material or issues within the online interaction. Without proficiency in these features, the exchange between practitioner and client would become impersonal and impracticable. The practitioner is required actively to demonstrate their understanding and attunement with a client, using skills which are adapted from those apparent in face-to-face encounters, in conjunction with seeking to establish and convey an online presence which instils a sense of trust within clients. It is vital that clients experience a feeling of being valued and heard. There will be distinct differences in how each client presents on a personal level, in addition to how their personal material, dialogue, and narrative style are conveyed within the context of CMC. Consideration of these points will assist practitioners in achieving attunement with their clients.

Points for consideration

- How do you currently communicate interest, attention, and attunement within face-to-face encounters? Consider how this could be transferred into CMC.
- What key issues would be apparent within differing platforms of CMC, which are additional to those illustrated within this section, and may impact upon securing attunement and the appropriate listening skills when engaging online with clients?
- What do you anticipate might influence your personal tendencies towards stereotyping or prejudicial reactions when encountering diversity within your engagement with online clients?

References

Greenberg, L., Rice, L. and Elliott, R. (1993) *Facilitating Emotional Change: The Moment-by-Moment Process*. New York: Guilford Press. p. 20.

Kraus, R., Zack, J. and Stricker, G. (2004) *Online Counselling: A Handbook for Mental Health Professionals*. London: Elsevier. p. 6.

Lago, C. and Smith, B. (2003) *Anti-Discriminatory Counselling Practice*. London: Sage. p. 13.

Magnavita, J. (2004) *Handbook of Personality Disorders*. Chichester: Wiley. p. 543.

Multi Cultural Issues Board (1996) Cultural Differences in Communication and Learning Styles. Available at http://www.asha.org/about/leadership-projects/multicultural/readings/.

Multi Cultural Issues Board (2005) *Cultural Difference in Communication and Learning Style*. American Speech-Language-Hearing Association. Available at www.asha.org/about/leadership-projects/multicultural/readings/reading_2.htm.

Murphy, L. and Mitchell, D. (1998) 'When writing helps to heal: email as therapy', *British Journal of Guidance & Counselling*, 26 (1): 21–32.

Nelson-Jones, R. (2003) *Basic Counselling Skills: A Helpers Manual*. London: Sage. p. 101.

Nelson-Jones, R. (2005) *Practical Counselling and Helping Skills*. London: Sage. p. 88.

Suler, J. and Fenichel, M. (2000) *Assessing a Person's Suitability for Online Therapy: Clinical Case Study Group Findings*. International Society for Mental Health Online. Available at www.ismho.org/builder//?p=page&id=222.

Wootton, R., Yellowlees, P. and McLaren, P. (2003) *Telepsychiatry and e-Mental Health*. London: RSM Press. p. 176.

Further reading, references, resources, and skill development activities relating to the subject matter within this chapter can be sourced via the companion website to this book.

5 ESTABLISHING AND MAINTAINING AN OPEN DIALOGUE

Online counselling skills presented in this chapter:

- Seeking clarification in online communication
- The use of questions within online supportive interactions
- The skill of paraphrasing and summarising within an online context
- Working with client resistance and non-verbal cues
- Offering challenges and feedback when working online
- How to manage misunderstandings and conflict in online communication
- The skill of online immediacy
- Self-disclosure in online working

Exercises and vignettes are included within this chapter, demonstrating the skills in practice and encouraging thought on the subject matter discussed.

This chapter presents the skills that are necessary from the onset of communicating online with clients, as they provide a 'dialogue pathway' whilst also being essential to the process of maintaining a continuous pathway throughout the course of the online relationship or interaction.

Seeking clarification in online communication

From the point of first contact with a client, there will be an amount of available information which may assist in forming an image of the client and promote an understanding of their presenting issues. Clients are often unsure of how much detail to provide during the early stages of interaction, and may also feel cautious regarding revealing in-depth personal information. It is therefore beneficial if the practitioner provides guidelines for clients in order to acquire sufficient detail to provide a foundation for establishing helpful and insightful communication.

Both during the beginning of the online relationship and at points throughout the interaction, there may be occasions where important information is omitted by clients or is presented in an ambiguous or biased manner. Where this does occur, clients may have chosen not to disclose information, or have not felt it relevant to do so. There may also be a personal interpretation of circumstances presented that is biased towards their understanding or experience, rather than providing a more general overview. There may be an absence of visual indicators which could provide a deeper sense of why this is so. Online intuition is a skill required of the practitioner, and develops with time through the experience acquired from working with a variety of clients from differing backgrounds, personal circumstances, gender, culture, and so on. Such online intuition guides the practitioner in how to seek clarification or challenge the absence of helpful or important information in conjunction with a client's personal bias towards issues presented. There are specific online counselling skills which can assist in the process of seeking clarification, whilst also expanding the potential for the practitioner's understanding of the presenting issues. This includes the careful phrasing of questions alongside the use of paraphrasing and summarising.

The use of questions within online supportive interactions

Online exchanges may not provide the opportunity to have visual and physical indicators or cues that can provide a sense of how a question has been received. When asking a question, a client may not have understood the manner in which the practitioner has phrased their question, or the content of it. This may lead to the client feeling confused or uncertain how to respond. In both synchronous and asynchronous contexts, this may create delays in a practitioner receiving a reply as re-wording of the question or clarification will be required. This may cause the client to feel reluctant to form a reply. Clients may also question how in tune the practitioner is with them as an individual and their presenting issues.

A further consideration is the variation in how a question will be audibly received in a verbal context, as opposed to how it is visually received when in a written form. Within an auditory setting, a direct question can be 'softened' or 'hardened' by the tone of voice and accentuation of certain words in conjunction with a visual presentation, using body language and eye contact. This can be a more difficult skill to develop within synchronous computer-mediated exchanges, as the flow of online interaction does not provide a practitioner with the same level of time for consideration and reflection as is available in asynchronous situations. The feature of writing a sentence, as opposed to verbalising it, requires additional time and may place added pressures upon the practitioner.

It is usual practice within a face-to-face counselling or supportive interaction to apply the use of open questions with the prefixes how, why, what, which, and when, as a tool in securing a comprehensive and specific response from a client. If such words are used in an online context without an initial 'softener', they can be experienced as too direct. It is beneficial to include additional wording, as this provides a more gentle approach to seeking information and responses from a client. Examples of this practice can be found throughout the simulated practitioner replies provided in each chapter of Part I of this book, with a more specific illustration of this practice provided by the examples below.

Phrasing open questions without undue directness

You will note that each example begins with a preliminary introduction or summary as a 'softener'.

1. It would be helpful to me in understanding the issue you have mentioned if you could tell me *how* …
2. I am gaining a sense of what this means to you, but I feel I could understand further if you were to tell me *what* …
3. There feels like there are a number of points which you have discussed and I believe I could respond in a more detailed way if you were able to tell me *why* you …
4. You have mentioned that you experience high levels of anxiety – can you explain to me *when* you …
5. You have talked about a number of experiences relating to your dyslexia – can you tell me *which* …

The inclusion of additional wording does take more time to consider and construct. It can also place greater emphasis on the pressures of time management when synchronously engaging with clients. When communicating asynchronously, this may also be a feature, as practitioners will be governed by time restrictions on forming responses to clients. Practitioners will develop a personalised style of forming questions when communicating online, based upon what feels natural to their style of online dialogue.

ⒺⓍⒺⓇⒸⒾⓈⒺ   ⑤.①

PHRASING ONLINE QUESTIONS

Within a personal or professional setting, you may have engaged in both synchronous and asynchronous exchanges with friends or colleagues where questions have been phrased to you with or without a 'softening' introduction. Take some time to reflect on how you experienced this, and also on how it may have influenced your response to the other person(s). How might this influence your skill development in formulating online question phrasing during online interactions?

The skill of paraphrasing and summarising within an online context

The online practitioner may experience some time pressures when using the skill of paraphrasing or summarising of narrative content and meaning of a client's interaction. This is due to such features taking longer to construct than when conveyed in verbal situations.

The skills of paraphrasing and summarising in an online setting require the formulation of a more précised arrangement, in order to provide space for the inclusion of other important elements and skills and the effective use of time resources (Kraus et al., 2004).

Online paraphrasing

Usually, within a face-to-face perspective, client material is presented verbally and the practitioner processes and 'stores' the dialogue as the meeting progresses. Where relevant, the practitioner will draw upon threads of the dialogue to present back as a means of providing a sense to the client that they have been 'heard', whilst also checking if the information the practitioner has 'stored' is accurate. The process of paraphrasing also allows a client to 'hear' the content of their dialogue as a further conceptual context to having spoken it. This can often initiate a client holding a different interpretation or experiencing of material they have presented. It is a very important aspect of a client gaining personal insight and moving forward with personal material presented within a face-to-face interaction, and as such is a necessary facet within online communication. Practitioners who are familiar with face-to-face supportive exchanges will have developed the skill of mentally holding relevant verbal information and presenting it back to a client when required.

For the online practitioner, there is a requirement to develop the skill of processing and storing written information and narrative, holding it in mind prior to presenting it back to a client in a written format. The development of this skill and the expertise in using it will depend on the individual's ability to hold and recount written information. Some practitioners may have a natural aptitude for this process, whilst others will require practice and experience to achieve competency.

Online summarising

In a face-to-face context, the use of summarising may feature at intervals as relevant to the content of a session and the needs or requirements of the client. There will usually be a summary at the ending of the session to consolidate any important elements that have been discussed or explored. A summary might also include points where either the practitioner or client has agreed to undertake a task following the session, or prior to the following meeting. Summarising holds an important feature within online interactions, particularly as misunderstanding or misinterpretation may occur due to the absence of advantages which are present in face-to-face working. This may be evident within group work situations, as discussion topics can move on very quickly and inhibit the opportunity to summarise all features of the members' discussion. Practitioners and clients may find it helpful to follow up a synchronous meeting with a brief asynchronous summary exchange of what was discussed within a session as an aid to clarify where misunderstandings may have occurred. An example of summarising within a simulated asynchronous practitioner reply can be found in Box 5.2. The middle section of the reply provides a summary of what the practitioner believes she has understood as the main issues presented by the simulated client example in Box 5.1.

Summarising in the manner provided within Box 5.2 can be particularly beneficial where:

- a client has not been specific in their communication regarding what they are seeking as a main focus of support from the practitioner; and
- where there is a large number of factors presented and it would be beneficial to draw them together in order for the client to clarify if the practitioner's perception of these are correct.

Often this process will generate a response from a client where they have structured a reply based upon key presenting issues which they feel are relevant, whilst omitting aspects of the practitioner's summary which are not experienced as relevant to the client or necessitating an immediate response. Where this occurs, the practitioner may decide to hold this in mind in the event that the relevance of previously presented subject matter becomes apparent in further communication from the client.

🄴🅇🄴🅁🄲🄸🅂🄴   🄵.🄶

RETAINING INFORMATION

Consider what current skills you have for retaining written narrative over a period of online exchanges in a personal or work context. How might such skills be further developed to promote your ability to paraphrase and summarise material from online exchanges?

Working with client resistance and non-verbal cues

Clarification of the term 'client resistance'

A client may not have initially provided a detailed illustration of themselves or the presenting issues they wish to cover in the online interaction. This may be due to feeling unsure regarding how much information to provide, or a resistance to disclose certain information. Evidence of resistance may continue to be apparent at times throughout the online relationship, which in turn will hinder the process of insight required to facilitate a positive outcome. Client resistance may be unconscious and originate from defence mechanisms which are well established and have been serving a beneficial purpose to the client. It is therefore important to note where resistance is evident and take time to consider the underlying motivation or cause. Research in a therapeutic setting indicates that there may be two main reasons why defences are apparent within the dialogue and relationship of a counsellor and client:

- the client may be blocking therapeutic insight or change due to seeking avoidance of anxiety, guilt, shame, or assuming responsibility for therapeutic change; and
- to repress uncomfortable feelings, memories, or personal responsibility for outcomes of situations.

A further cause of resistance may be due to the client feeling that the practitioner has misunderstood them, or has offered an interpretation or intervention which is wrong. Aspects of resistance can occur when a client's sense of reality is distorted and the resulting inappropriate behaviour is a product of the client's distorted reality (Hall, 2003).

Such resistance may have been constructed over a period of time, even years, as an adopted coping strategy against insight to 'self' or perception of 'self' in the context of relationships with others. Practitioners should be more tentative with challenging potential resistance in the early stages of the online relationship. Having an established and solid online relationship with a client provides the increased potential for a successful outcome, as there will be a foundation to support the level of anxiety which such interventions can evoke in a client. Challenge or confronting of a client's internal frame of reference should always be carefully considered and not overdone: too many challenges may actually generate resistance (Nelson-Jones, 2003).

Working in an online context, particularly in a non-synchronous exchange, limits the opportunity to gauge how a challenge to resistance is being received by the client, whilst also making it more difficult to avoid the possibility of causing irreparable damage to the relationship. Working synchronously can provide greater opportunity to sense how the challenge of a resistance has been received and find a positive way forward from that point. Asynchronous challenges can be approached sensitively using a variation of approach; an example of this is provided in Box 5.1, where Sam has written an email to Julie following the previous synchronous meeting.

Box 5.1* Working with client resistance

Hi Julie,

I'm glad you suggested the live meeting as I feel it helped me to be more relaxed about talking. I'd like to say more about other things which have happened over the last three years. My partner left me after a four-year relationship. I feel upset with him as I discovered that he had been having an affair during the last year we were together. I knew that he didn't love me during the last two years that we were together and wasn't committed to the relationship, but at the time it was easier to let things carry on the way they were as I didn't want to go through with a separation. I had always wanted another child, even before we had met, but he said he wasn't ready for that commitment and was always angry with me when I approached the subject. I did think about the possibility of becoming pregnant against his wishes. I feel that I wasted so much time with the relationship when it was obvious that it wasn't going to work and also it's made things so difficult with my eldest daughter as she was very close to him and unhappy about the separation.

Hopefully you can help me to move on from this so I can find another chance to be happy and gain back the trust I once had from my daughter...............

In the email illustrated in Box 5.1, it is apparent that the client is resistant in considering any personal responsibility for the outcome of the relationship with her ex-partner and the current difficulties with her daughter. She appears to have shifted the responsibility upon her ex-partner. Such bias, when providing background to the presenting issues, could be interpreted in a variety of ways and would therefore affect the content of a reply, particularly in relation to challenging any apparent resistance to acknowledge personal responsibility for the current outcome of the client's relationship and her daughter's behaviour since the separation.

When engaging with clients in a face-to-face context, practitioners may decide to mildly challenge any apparent resistance within the first meeting, due to having the opportunity to sense how the client is responding to such an intervention. They would also be in a position to recover any visible signs of the client withdrawing. When conducting an online practice, particularly when using an asynchronous medium, opportunities to have access to such indications are more limited and therefore resistance should be challenged more tentatively.

Box 5.2*   Challenging Sam's resistance

Hi Sam,

Thank you for your email. I'm pleased you felt that the live meeting helped you in feeling more comfortable to look at further issues you would like me to support you with.

It feels as though you are going through a difficult time in relation to various aspects of your life at the moment. Some of which you indicate are directly related to the relationship ending and others which impact on you in a more general way, such as your wish to have a further child. In your email you expressed how upset you feel towards your partner regarding the affair and your feelings regarding the relationship being a waste of time. I sense that you are angry with him due to your hope of having a further child being quashed by his ending of the relationship…………..

From reading your email I have a sense that the issues and circumstances you are finding difficult to manage and those you would like to focus on within our online sessions fall into the following areas:

The ending of your relationship, which you feel was brought about by your partner having an affair.

Your intent to have another child, which has been halted by the relationship ending.

Your decision to remain in the relationship, although you were aware that your partner no longer loved you. This choice being made due to you not feeling able to make the decision to end the relationship, as you hoped your partner would change his mind about having a child.

Your feelings of having wasted time by staying in the relationship when you couldn't see a long-term future together with the relationship as it was.

> I have a sense that you feel the basis of your choice to stay in the relationship has been taken away from you by your partner being unfaithful and ending the relationship, and this has left you feeling angry with him, but open to seeking a way to move forward on your own.
>
> You mention that you would like support in finding personal happiness. I wondered if it might help to explore where you feel you may have made choices during the relationship, which upon reflection could have prevented you from gaining personal happiness and may also have impacted on others who were close to your partner............

The email reply in Box 5.2 offers a subtle challenge to the client's resistance with the intent of encouraging thought and insight to where Sam may have contributed to her unhappiness in the relationship and the outcome. Such summaries reiterate the main points raised by the client whilst endeavouring to phrase it in a manner which encourages the client to 'hear' where she had made choices which influenced the outcome. Where a client does not include reflection upon a subtle challenge in subsequent emails, and it becomes apparent that they are still experiencing 'blind spots' in awareness, it would be advisable to offer further summarisation at a suitable opportunity.

If engaging with a client in asynchronous communication does not provide the opportunity to overcome apparent resistance, it may be beneficial to suggest that the client considers supplementing asynchronous meetings with a synchronous meeting. This can provide a variation in opportunity to explore resistance and unconscious defence mechanisms which may be impacting upon the level of insight achieved by the client.

EXERCISE 5.3

ADDRESSING CLIENT RESISTANCE

Consider how you might form a response to the simulated client example provided in Box 5.1. How would you interpret and challenge any apparent resistance within the content of the client email? How might your summarising of client material have differed to that demonstrated in Box 5.2?

Non-verbal cues

The absence of a physical presence in online encounters limits opportunities to notice and work with non-verbal cues such as facial expression, body language, dress or personal care, and so on. Anthony (2000) stresses that attention to how a client presents themselves in text format is key to developing rapport. Colon (1996) identifies the use of emotional bracketing as one of the valuable tools for assisting in conveying non-verbal cues.

Compensation for the loss of verbal and auditory cues can be achieved by adopting the use of person-centred core conditions, including empathy, warmth, congruence, and unconditional positive regard. Computer-mediated communication (CMC) will often generate individual and personalised non-verbal client cues which the practitioner can utilise to inform their understanding of clients and their presenting issues. They may also be developed by clients to become a sophisticated personalised art form (Kraus et al., 2004). Such cues can provide insight to a client's current, emotional, and physical well-being and provide the opportunity for supportive exploration relating to underlying issues or concerns. This is particularly helpful where there are visible changes in client presentation over a number of online meetings.

When interacting with a client during a one-off session, or a brief period of exchanges, it may be more difficult to pick up on non-verbal cues. There may be benefits for some clients, where they are not in the physical presence of a practitioner, as the anonymity of online exchanges can assist in promoting a heightened focus of self-expression without aspects of self-consciousness that face-to-face interactions can evoke (Goss and Anthony, 2003). This being accepted, one could assume that there is less likelihood of the relevance of non-verbal cues within online working as the medium itself alleviates feelings which initiate non-verbal cues.

Non-verbal cues may be highlighted in any of the following variations, in addition to individual client nuances, which the helper will become aware of as the online interaction develops:

- The use of different fonts to those normally contained within emails.
- Colour variation to text.
- Variation in layout or presentation of an email.
- Change in use of avatar or symbol used in other synchronous mediums.
- The use of acronyms and emoticons.
- Introducing text in capitals or within inverted commas, brackets, and so on, where this had not been previously used by the client.
- Communication becoming briefer than usual, less frequent, not maintaining contact as agreed, or written text becoming less/more coherent.
- A variation in written expression of feeling, memories, personal awareness.
- A client's regular use of personalised communication style (including words, phrases, writing style, and so on) which can illustrate themes in non-verbal cues.

🄴🅇🄴🅁🄲🄸🅂🄴   🄵.🄴

ONLINE CUES

Consider what additional online features may indicate non-verbal cues being apparent within online presentations.

Working with online non-verbal cues

An example of online non-verbal cues is provided in Box 5.3, where the simulated client work with Sam is developed to introduce a further email exchange. It is apparent when comparing the structure, style and content of Box 5.1 and Box 5.3 that there are indications of variations in how the client has constructed her email, which give the helper insight to non-verbalised cues and change within the client interaction and her internal thought processes.

Box 5.3*   Working with non-verbal cues

Hi Julie ☺…

I found your comments really helpful in thinking about what had happened over the last few months (and last 2 years) I hadn't realised there were so many aspects to how I was feeling until I saw them laid out in the email. It was also helpful to see it in point form as it helped me to separate out the different issues which I feel unhappy about. I guess this helped me to understand why I've been feeling so tense and angry since my partner left. It also feels good that I can say **I am angry with him**!!!! (Particularly as he was never comfortable with me being angry)

I do feel that my partner made most of the choices in our relationship, although I went along with most due to hoping that it would help in him agreeing to have a child. I think I can see where I may have made some choices which were not helpful to me… and I feel uncomfortable about that now. I'm really not sure how I could have done anything different about it though, but perhaps I need to think about that more if I don't want to end up in the same situation in the future…………….

In the example provided in Box 5.3, it is apparent that the client has become more relaxed with the practitioner and uses a smiling face emoticon at the beginning of the email. This simple online expression can offer useful insight into the possibilities of how the relationship can be further enhanced and developed. Within online exchanges, it is important to respond to the openness that has been conveyed by a client. To ignore such an invitation could be experienced as a rebuff and potentially damage the developing therapeutic process of the work.

The practitioner's understanding and interpretation of non-verbalised anger in the client's first email (Box 5.1), and the acknowledgement of this in the reply (Box 5.2), invited the client to express anger explicitly in reply (Box 5.3). Assisting a client to identify feelings, through the helper's interpretation of non-verbal cues, can help the therapeutic process to move forward, whilst also encouraging a client to be confident in using explicit feeling expression in future exchanges.

The client's use of bracketing in the reply contained within Box 5.3 indicates that she is feeling more confident in sharing her internal thought processes without fear of being judged in a negative manner. When forming replies, it is helpful to use a similar style to that adopted by the client. This demonstrates the practitioner's internal thoughts, whilst also endeavouring to develop a symbiotic element to the relationship. Symbiosis is a strong feature within face-to-face supportive work as a mechanism for a client to feel they are valued and integral to the relationship (Jacobs, 2006).

Suggesting clients engage with a combination of synchronous and asynchronous meetings can also highlight non-verbal cues which may not be so apparent when communicating by one medium alone. This may be more relevant when supplementing asynchronous communication with synchronous exchanges. The feature of immediacy is more evident in this context as an increased opportunity exists for spontaneous responses, in conjunction with having the opportunity to experience any apparent 'silences' which a client initiates. An example of this during synchronous engagement may be where a client seems to 'disappear' for a few seconds. There may be a variety of reasons for this occurring, including clients pausing to answer the door to visitors, answering the telephone, pausing to gather their thoughts, and feeling overcome by feelings evoked by the subject matter being discussed. Such non-verbal cues would not be apparent when communicating via email or other asynchronous interaction, and require careful consideration by the online practitioner in how to respond.

Offering challenges and feedback when working online

I would like to clarify that my use of the word 'challenge' should be taken in a therapeutic context, as opposed to a more general use of the word. In a supportive counselling context, such an intervention represents encouraging exploration of client material or thought processes, with the intention of facilitating a clarification of presented material or supporting personal insight for a client. Challenge should also be introduced with the aim of enhancing the work, not as a means of introducing a personal agenda of the helper. In the same manner, the offering of feedback to a client, and the content of the feedback, should be carefully considered, as an inappropriate or ambiguous intonation could have a negative impact on the potential to achieve a positive outcome (Sutton and Stewart, 2002).

The 'sandwich' analogy, which is often used within the structuring and content of face-to-face feedback, can be applied to an online context. Start with a positive offering to a client in order to gain their attention and reinforce their belief that you have good intention, offer the feedback in a non-judgemental or critical manner, and finally leave the recipient with a choice in being able to seek clarification and the freedom to apply any suggestions intended within the rationale of the feedback.

How to manage misunderstandings and conflict in online communication

There is the potential for destructive miscommunication to occur within online interactions, due the disadvantage of not having the physical presence of a client and their auditory and visual cues to assess where a misunderstanding may have occurred (Childress, 1998). The absence of body language and visual and auditory indicators restricts the practitioner's access to being alert or having access to the same resources that are available in resolving potential and actual misunderstandings or conflict.

Munro (2002) highlights the increased evidence of projections within online interactions. This is due to interpretations of communication being formed through the individual's perceptions. Such interpretations may be related to expectations, needs, fantasies, feelings, and desires and are subsequently projected onto those who a person is interacting with. The written narrative received during online exchanges is not heard in an auditory sense, but purely 'heard' in one's own head and therefore interpreted in a manner which does not necessarily reflect the tone or meaning intended by the sender. The online practitioner's skill lies in precisely conveying the tone, meaning, and intent of their communication.

Moussou and White (2004) refer to five considerations which are relevant to those who communicate and interact online. Practitioners should therefore be aware of and reflect upon these during the process of online communication. Assumptions are a natural feature of any interpersonal communication and are influenced by personal experiences, attitudes, gender, faith, and so on. It is particularly pertinent to check out such assumptions when supporting others online, as there may be an increased likelihood of this resulting in conflict. Using a prefix such as 'I' as opposed to 'you', which is the same practice when using counselling skills in a face-to-face interaction, is essential. The skill of active listening, which is key to avoidance of assumption, is demonstrated by other pointers than those used in face-to-face interactions and require textual indicators within online interactions; these skills are discussed in Chapter 4.

Resolving conflict in online helping or supportive interactions

Within online therapeutic or supportive interactions, there may be instances where a practitioner feels that they are unable to resolve the conflict. Even with repeated attempts to find a positive way forward, a decision may be reached to end the online interaction or relationship with a client. Dependent upon the variations in context of the practitioner's professional practice, this may lead to a client seeking a mediation process, or in some circumstances a client may request the support of a professional body to intervene on their behalf. A professional responsibility for those who conduct an online practice is an acceptance of consistently seeking to be proactive in minimising the potential for misunderstandings and conflict to arise in their client work. Where any such instances may arise, or become evident, practitioners have a responsibility to respond in a sensitive and supportive manner with the intention of achieving a constructive and affirming resolution for a client.

EXERCISE   5.5

RESPONDING TO ONLINE MISUNDERSTANDINGS

To assist in understanding how conflict or misunderstanding can arise through written or online communication, it may be helpful to reflect upon where you have received a letter or email which has evoked a negative reaction within you and caused you to feel aggrieved or angry towards the sender. You might also like to reflect on how you responded to this in both a negative or positive manner and the resulting outcome.

There are positive ways to approach the resolution of potential or actual conflict and may include utilising some or all of the guidelines detailed below.

Misunderstanding or conflict arising within asynchronous communication

Take some 'time out' before responding to any resulting conflict, particularly if this occurs early on in an online interaction, as you may not be fully familiar with the client's style of online presentation to determine whether the communication was intended in the way you have interpreted it. There are benefits to reading through the source of conflict more than once in order to seek clarification on the sender's intended tone. It may be that the communication evokes strong feeling and an urge to respond immediately, but it is better to wait and respond when the initial reaction has subsided a little. Ideally, the first point of reference for providing clarification where a misunderstanding has occurred will be the client. If the content of the communication appears ambiguous, then seek clarification from the client in a sensitive and constructive manner, specifically asking for clarification of the intended meaning. It may be that after requesting clarification, there is still an obvious conflict which requires resolution.

If you are receiving supervision for your online practice, seek the advice and support of your supervisor. If this resource is not available to you, you may wish to consider approaching a colleague who also works online, to provide assistance in gaining a 'third party' perspective. It might also be beneficial to ask the client to consider joining you in a synchronous meeting if possible, as this may increase the opportunity to seek clarification. It is always beneficial to bear in mind that a client may be unfamiliar with emotional expression in an online setting and that the source of misunderstanding or conflict may have been triggered without explicit intent. There may be occasions where a client is not familiar with appropriate online or face-to-face etiquette in conveying negative feelings and is not prepared to consider how they might more appropriately express themselves. If this is the case, it should be discussed with the client with the intention of seeking their cooperation in being referred to another forum of support.

Misunderstanding or conflict arising within synchronous communication

Within synchronous online communication, there may not be the advantage of having time for reflection prior to seeking clarification regarding misunderstandings or areas of conflict. The interaction takes place in real time and a lengthy pause to consider what has been conveyed prior to constructing a reply may add to any apparent tension which is evident for either party. The advantage within synchronous online communication is having the opportunity to seek a resolution in 'real' time and being in a position to move forward without the same time delay which occurs in asynchronous exchanges. The practitioner should be mindful of the potential for spontaneity within synchronous working which could prove to be advantageous or detrimental in these circumstances.

Resolving difficulties where a practitioner has caused a misunderstanding or conflict

There is the likelihood that a practitioner may unintentionally cause a reciprocal process of conflict for a client. With the absence of physical presence, it is more difficult to assess where this may have occurred, unless the client feels able or empowered to identify it. It is therefore pertinent for the practitioner to consistently monitor how they present their online narrative and pay attention to the tone and intonation of their communication.

Where a practitioner makes an intervention which holds the potential to evoke a negative response from a client, or where there is a sense that this may have actually occurred, the practitioner should check with the client how they have 'received' the intervention and offer the opportunity to provide feedback. In such cases, the practitioner should provide clarification and consider rephrasing the communication. For those practitioners who have trained in face-to-face counselling skills, you will be familiar with the manner in which to own your feedback, using the word 'I' in place of generalised terms such as 'you' or 'we' and so on. It is also important to use the counselling skill of feeling expression when intending to seek clarification or convey how you have experienced a statement. Offering affirmative statement reassurances to the client, as shown in Case example 5.1, may also assist in maintaining a positive dialogue.

Case example 5.1

Affirmative statements in feedback

I feel you are working very hard to convey your support needs to me, but in your last email reply I sensed that I may have said something previously which you have misunderstood, or do not agree with........can we discuss this in order to clarify what my intent was and also to offer a reassurance that it was put forward with a positive intention. I hope you feel able to discuss this as I believe it will help if there are any future areas of our communication where a misunderstanding arises.

It is advisable to provide information to potential clients relating to the likelihood of misunderstandings arising prior to them engaging with online support. Such guidance can clearly outline for a client the etiquette for both parties in seeking clarification and a positive resolution. There may be occasions where a positive resolution cannot be reached, and this could result in a client seeking mediation or choosing to lodge a complaint against a practitioner or the online service. In either instance, clients should be provided with this information via the website of the service, or have it made available to them during the contracting phase of the online interaction/relationship.

ⒺⓍⒺⓡⓒⓘⓢⓔ ⑤.⑥

RESPONDING TO ONLINE CONFLICT

Consider how you currently respond to, and manage, misunderstandings or conflict within face-to-face client interactions. How might these skills be developed and transferred into circumstances where conflict may occur within online client interactions?

The skill of online immediacy

As when deploying the use of counselling skills within in a face-to-face context, the use of immediacy holds a similar relevance with computer-mediated exchanges. Wosket (1999) indicates that using immediacy is a way of conveying genuineness and being transparent with a client. The use of immediacy may be less spontaneous when working through asynchronous communication, and may not hold the opportunity to gauge how the intervention has been received by the client. When seeking to include immediacy in online interactions, it is beneficial to supplement asynchronous communication with synchronous exchanges, as this can provide the opportunity for the inclusion of immediacy and a client gaining an increased sense of the practitioner's presence and spontaneity (Kraus et al., 2004).

Collie et al. (2001) refer to the term 'descriptive immediacy' to define a way of increasing the connection between a helper and client. Such interventions are used to illustrate the intensity of emotion when a simple verbal response may not be sufficient to convey the feelings being experienced. Descriptive immediacy can also be used to convey a deeper level of engagement with a client prior to offering a challenge to inconsistency in client-presented material.

Case example 5.2

Descriptive immediacy in an asynchronous reply to a client

I am really struck by how your recent promotion at work has helped you to feel more confident. I am sitting here with a very strong image of you being informed of the promotion. When I picture this I feel very proud for your achievement. If we were working in a face-to-face session now you would see a big smile on my face, and my arms in an open gesture to demonstrate that I feel you have reached a very significant point in overcoming the obstacles of the last few months.

Such an offering of descriptive immediacy as shown in Case example 5.2 can convey a sense of a practitioner's presence to a client and hold the potential to enhance and strengthen the online relationship. Although conveyed through asynchronous communication, this can elicit an image of the practitioner and their congruent experiencing of the client's email.

Self-disclosure in online working

Professional disclosure

The previous illustration, which referred to descriptive immediacy, leads quite aptly into the subject of self-disclosure. The disinhibition dynamic which is evident within online interactions is likely to increase the incidences of client self-disclosure, and may also hold implications for practitioners to be susceptible to increased disclosure. Disclosure within the context of professional online practice will be particularly pertinent to the promotion of an online service. Clients will not have the usual reassurances that are available with the setting of face-to-face support. This would include being able to validate the identity, qualifications, and location of the practitioner or service. It is common practice for therapists and other professionals to display actual copies of certification and affiliation or accreditation to professional bodies within their office as a reassurance to clients that they are receiving a service from a bona fide practitioner. It is therefore a professional necessity that online practitioners impart detailed information relating to their experience, qualifications, and any professional bodies they are affiliated to, and where requested offer reassurances to clients by providing copies of their qualifications, and so on.

In order to gain an empathic understanding of the dilemma a client may face when considering online support, you may wish to reflect on instances where you had considered purchasing a service or product from the Internet, but have held reservations in doing so because there was limited visual and textual information to convince you that you were purchasing an item which sufficiently fitted your needs. Most potential 'customers' in any context seek a personal and straightforward service, alongside being able to gain a sense that they can trust in being responded to by a reputable and reliable service provider. The process of a client seeking online support will naturally fall into a similar requirement.

ⒺⓍⒺⓇⒸⒾⓈⒺ   ⑤.⑦

OFFERING ONLINE REASSURANCE

What reassurances would you want to offer online clients, and how could this be achieved within your online practice?

Personal disclosure

Within the practice of face-to-face counselling and supportive working, there is a wide variation in views regarding the appropriateness of self-disclosure and the benefit or disadvantage this may bring to client work. Personal disclosure in either a face-to-face or online context should be given on the basis that it would enhance the therapeutic nature of the work with a client, as opposed to any personal gain. With the loss of a physical presence, a client may seek more personal information and disclosure from a practitioner than would usually be sought within face-to-face professional services. Where this occurs, the decision to proceed should be reviewed in light of the previous statement.

In all instances, it is important to consider why you as practitioner are considering greater personal self-disclosure than previously deemed appropriate within the general context of supportive working, in conjunction with the potential benefits/disadvantages of doing so.

Summary

This chapter has discussed how a practitioner can actively seek to establish and maintain an open dialogue with their clients. There are an extensive number of skills required in order to achieve this when interacting with clients using CMC. The primary responsibility for achieving a clear and constructive dialogue pathway lies with the practitioner in their role as facilitator of the online inter-action or relationship. The majority of such skills are conveyed in the explicit narrative or dialogue with a client. The remainders are formed by the practi-tioner paying close attention to undertones or nuances which they sense are evi-dent within what is being explicitly expressed by the client, or is sensed from unspoken dynamics that are more intangible in presentations by a client.

Effective online interaction will necessitate a practitioner developing all of the skills required in an adapted form to that which applies in a face-to-face interaction. The absence of a physical presence leaves a practitioner with less palpable indications or evidence of a client having engaged with the online interaction and the practitioner, whilst also making it difficult at times to establish and maintain a level of communication where both parties feel heard and understood. Where a practitioner senses or becomes explicitly aware that assumptions or misunderstandings have occurred within an online interaction, it is beneficial to seek clarification and a positive resolution as soon as practi-cally possible, with full consideration to the client and the positive benefits in resolving any emerging or evident difficulties within the online communication.

Points for consideration

- When reviewing relevant skills for securing information via verbal ques-tions, what further development is required to concisely secure required information when communicating in an online context?
- How might an online practitioner's approach to working with resistance and non-verbal cues be influenced by the cultural orientation of clients?
- What are your initial thoughts regarding online mediation and conflict res-olution? How can features of face-to-face practice for conflict resolution and client grievances be successfully transferred or adapted to CMC?

References

Anthony, K. (2000) 'Counselling in Cyberspace', *Counselling*, 11 (10): 625–7.

Childress, C. (1998) *Potential Risks and Benefits of Online Psychotherapeutic Interventions*. Available at www.ismho.org/issues/9801.htm.

Collie, K., Mitchell, D. and Murphy, L. (2001) *E-Mail Counselling: Skills for Maximum Impact*. Eric/CASS Digest. Available at www.ericdigests.org/2002-3/e-mail.htm.

Colon, Y. (1996) 'Chatter(er)ing through the fingertips: doing group therapy online. Women and performance', *Journal of Feminist Theory*, 9: 205–215.

Goss, S. and Anthony, K. (2003) *Technology in Counselling and Psychotherapy. A Practitioner's Guide*. Basingstoke: Palgrave. p. 42.

Hall, C. (ed.) (2003) *Constructing Clienthood in Social Work and Human Services: Interaction, Identities and Practices*. London: Jessica Kingsley. p. 196.

Jacobs, M. (2006) *Presenting Past: An Introduction to Practical Psychodynamic Counselling*. Maidenhead: McGraw-Hill Open University Press.

Kraus, R., Zack, J. and Stricker, G. (2004) *Online Counselling: A Handbook for Mental Health Professionals*. San Diego, CA: Elsevier/Academic Press. pp. 9, 22.

Moussou, M. and White, N. (2004) *Avoiding Online Conflict*. Available at www.fullcirc.com/community/avoidingconflict.htm.

Munro, K. (2002) *Conflict in Cyberspace: How to Resolve Conflict Online*. Available at www-usr.rider.edu/~suler/psycyber/conflict.html.

Nelson-Jones, R. (2003) *Basic Counselling Skills: A Helper's Guide*. London: Sage. p. 88.

Sutton, J. and Stewart, W. (2002) *Learning to Counsel*. Oxford: How to Books.

Wosket, V. (1999) *The Therapeutic Use of Self*. New York: Routledge. p. 51.

Further reading, references, resources, and skill development activities relating to the subject matter within this chapter can be sourced via the companion website to this book.

PART II

Professional Considerations

Welcome to Part II of this book, which provides an in-depth illustration of the integral aspects required when structuring a professional online practice. This part also provides guidance for both organisations and practitioners seeking to develop and enhance their online presence and adherence to ethical and legal practice.

In addition to the practical skills defined in Part I, which are required to establish and maintain effective communication and online relationships with clients, the skills and considerations outlined in this section are key features to the overall quality, structure, and effectiveness of service delivery.

Chapter 6 defines the processes involved in online assessment and contracting which is apparent in all variations of professional activity where computer-mediated technology is adopted for engaging with clients. The process of assessment and contracting within a general context requires specialist skills and is particularly relevant to therapeutic or mental health settings. When conducted through an online medium, the absence of physical characteristics and representations, such as those available in a face-to-face meeting, necessitate a different approach. The content of this chapter presents guidance on methods for successfully implementing online assessment procedures.

Chapter 7 encourages the reader to reflect upon the professional considerations apparent within this field of practice and explores the relevance of seeking individual supervision and peer support, which is integral to the process of evaluating and developing insight to client work whilst also a strategic process in the progression of skill and knowledge development.

Chapter 8 serves as a reference point for readers to utilise for ensuring that their intended or current practice complies with the ethical and professional requirements for online practice. The content of this chapter draws together key points from both Parts I and II in the form of concise guidelines for effective practice.

Finally, the Conclusion discusses aspects relating to current and future developments within this field of practice, including the relevance of immediate issues which are proposed as necessary features for promoting a wider understanding and the significance of computer-mediated engagement with clients.

Throughout Part II, each chapter contains exercises, examples, and points for consideration. These features encourage further thought by the practitioner relating to relevant factors which are required to develop and implement a service provision when adopting the use of online counselling skills.

Further reading, references, resources, and skills development activities are features of each chapter and can be sourced via the companion website to this book.

6 ONLINE ASSESSMENT AND CONTRACTING

Online counselling skill topics presented in this chapter:

- Client groups seeking online support: encompassing client needs
- Assessment procedures
- Contracting
- Online risk assessment
- Confidentiality
- Endings

Exercises and vignettes are included within this chapter, demonstrating the skills in practice and encouraging thought on the subject matter discussed.

This chapter provides insight to the process of assessment, contracting, and related matters, whilst also prompting thought which can assist practitioners and online service providers in formulating and implementing appropriate systems for service delivery and conclusions relating to professional practice. Amongst the many that are electing to engage with their clients online are UK Careers and Guidance services. Initial reports indicate that this holds the potential to be successful in either asynchronous or synchronous contact with clients (Madahar, 2004). With the increasing range of services now engaging with clients through online exchanges, there is a broad framework of practice in this field. This chapter provides insight and guidance across a spectrum of circumstances where practitioners connect in such a manner with clients, illustrating how assessment and contracting feature as an integral aspect to this sphere of professional practice. In each aspect of service delivery, there are underlying considerations which apply and will influence conclusions relating to the suitability of this medium for client groups and specific individual client presenting issues. Conducting an assessment without the physical presence of a client brings additional consideration due to:

- potential difficulties in substantiating background information; and
- systems required for determining the authenticity and suitability of an applicant for online support.

These points being noted, there may be distinct benefits in conducting assessment for both face-to-face and computer-mediated client services via online assessment resources, as this may assist with some of the inhibiting factors encountered during assessments conducted in the physical presence of a practitioner.

Some clients will seek to engage with practitioners where they have identified online support as offering a level of anonymity and distance which is not reciprocated in face-to-face encounters. It can therefore provide an opening for some clients to consider accessing specific areas of support where they might previously have felt reluctant or unable to do so. Not all such applications may be assessed as suitable to receiving support for a variety of reasons, and proceeding may prove to compound personal dynamics which would be more appropriately addressed in face-to-face interactions. The chapter will highlight the nature of how this may be presented by the inclusion of simulated case study examples.

Client groups seeking online support: encompassing client needs

The current movement of clients seeking online support

The advent of the Internet is providing opportunities for individuals and groups to engage in social, professional, and other personal interactions in an extended manner to those established as traditional forms of interaction. It is becoming commonplace for practitioners and their clients to engage with each other using computer-mediated communication (CMC). Assessment, contracting, and confidentiality are essential considerations in developing an effective and professional service to clients, and the manner in which this is included within service delivery will be influenced by the context of the practitioner's sphere of work.

Examples of the current areas where considerable online service development is taking place fall into the following categories, each of which uses various assessment systems to establish suitability of this medium for individuals within their client base:

- formal counselling and therapeutic practice providers
- supervision and consultation services
- life coaching and personal development
- youth agencies
- training services
- careers guidance services
- personal support agencies, such as befriending, and specific issue agencies, such as depression alliance and young minds and so on
- crisis support agencies such as the Samaritans and Befrienders International

- academic institutions
- employee assistance providers
- public and government service organisations
- pastoral and ministerial organisations
- community resources and support networks
- mental health and general health advice and support agencies.

EXERCISE 6.1

ADDITIONAL RESOURCES WHICH COULD BE TRANSFERRED INTO AN EFFECTIVE ONLINE SERVICE PROVISION

If you were considering seeking support from an online resource, which services would you feel comfortable accessing using an online medium, and what would be the rationale behind this?

What aspects relating to the online promotion of a service would most attract and encourage you to engage with the service?

Within your own sphere of practice and in a broader context, what online resources might clients require, and potentially be willing to engage with?

The suitability of an online medium to provide support for client groups

In all instances where service providers and practitioners are considering moving into providing online resources and support for their clients, it is beneficial to consider the following points in relation to suitability of the medium for client groups:

- Can the quality of service delivery be maintained and enhance the existing service provision?
- Will the introduction of such a facility restrict or directly disadvantage any existing or potential service users?
- Will alternative mediums of support still be available to those clients who do not wish to engage with an online practitioner?
- Can suitable referral procedures be established where online support is deemed as suitable for client needs?
- In areas where clients may present as high-risk of harm to themselves or others, can an online resource provide appropriate levels of support in the area of duty of care?

🄴🅇🄴🅁🄲🄸🅂🄴   🔢.🔢

SUITABILITY OF ONLINE SUPPORT

Consider what additional factors might influence the suitability
of online support for general use with client groups, and also
within your particular field of practice.

Assessment procedures

Client assessment – suitability of the medium for the individual client

In some instances, agencies may decide to proceed in engaging with clients
without conducting an initial assessment process, and have based such a
decision on a specific rationale or a remit of the facility offered to clients.
Where it has been decided that assessment forms an essential part of the
application process, and service delivery is not initiated until this has been
completed, the resulting outcomes will influence whether or not a service
can be offered to individual clients. Online practitioners have a responsibility to establish clear criteria relating to assessment procedures and identifying appropriate circumstances where online engagement is suited to their
client needs and presenting issues (Anthony and Jamieson, 2005;
Pergament, 1998).

In all such instances, decisions should be concluded with the intention of
securing a suitable and accessible resource for the client in conjunction with
relevant ethical issues apparent in this context of professional practice and
any evident legal and jurisdictional requirements (Suler and Fenichel, 2000).
In all instances where assessment is included in service delivery, the adopted
assessment tools should be fit for their purpose and regularly evaluated
(Kraus et al., 2004). There may be a variety of reasons why assessment outcomes conclude that it would not be appropriate to support clients using
computer-mediated support, and this may be based upon one or more of the
following factors where the client may:

- possess an insufficient level of computer literacy to gain the required input
  from the service or achieve a positive outcome
- have limited use of the language in which the service is offered
- present with disabilities which restrict effective access to support through
  an online medium
- demonstrate reluctance or show unwillingness to comply with contractual
  requirements of the service

- present to the service in a manner which indicates that appropriate duty of care cannot be provided
- present in a therapeutic context with personal issues, mental health issues, or disabilities which show contra-indications to online counselling being conducive to their emotional well-being or stability
- present to a service where legal stipulations indicate that client confidentiality could be compromised by the nature of presenting issues, or the practitioner may find themselves breaching legal requirements by proceeding.

In certain instances, assessment will feature as an ongoing process during the early stages of engaging with a client. An example of this may be where indications of the medium being unsuitable were evident at the point of first contact, although the contra-indications were insufficient to confirm unsuitability. It is important to inform the client that a process of continuing assessment is occurring and may lead to a referral if online exchanges are concluded to be unsuitable. Where an assessment decision is formed and concludes that online support is unsuitable for a client, an appropriate referral point should be offered and a full explanation provided to the client. There is an area of obvious advantage to a service in being able to offer both face-to-face and online support to clients.

Box 6.1 Client assessment

June applies to her university careers guidance service for online support in planning her academic progression into PhD study. She will shortly be engaged in placement activity and therefore located away from the locality of her current university. Following a brief exchange of emails where an informal assessment process is in process, the careers advisor offers June a series of online exchanges in which to explore the next stage of her academic study.

During the course of the first contracted exchanges, it becomes apparent that the work schedule of June's placement and inability to regularly access a computer to write her emails is resulting in disjointed communication. The frustration June is experiencing in maintaining consistent contact with the careers advisor is very apparent in her emails. The careers advisor was aware in the initial application to access the service that June will return to the university over the imminent Easter break and therefore suggests that face-to-face meetings may be more suited to June's needs based upon the current difficulties in maintaining contact. June agrees to visit the careers service at the appointment times offered, and feels a sense of relief not to continue with the level of anxiety and frustration she had experienced in trying to engage with the careers officer in online exchanges.

In the example provided in Box 6.1, it is apparent that although online exchanges with the practitioner were assessed as meeting the client's needs during the initial assessment process, it later became apparent that the client's placement circumstances were preventing her from gaining the level of inter-action she required to form her decision regarding PhD study. In this instance, the practitioner made an appropriate assessment decision and proceeded to offer the client the alternative of visiting the careers service, as it had become clear that an appropriate level of service delivery could not be maintained for the client given her current circumstances.

Online support as an adjunct to face-to-face interactions

In many contexts of providing face-to-face support, there may be the oppor-tunity to supplement or continue working with clients using an online medium, and there may be evident advantages to supplementing sessions in this manner (Kraus et al., 2004). Where this is the case, the following points will assist in forming an assessment decision on the relevance and suitability for this to be offered as a supplementary or transitional resource for clients:

- The client has sufficient computer and general literacy, communication skills, and experience with Internet technology to make the transition into online support.
- The client is willing to consider online support and is not being driven to consider the transition due to the practitioner's intent or personal benefits.
- The client is provided with an appropriate period of time to consider the proposal of adopting online communication with the practitioner.
- The benefits to the client in making the transition outweigh any evident disadvantages.
- A risk assessment has been undertaken relating to the client previously presenting issues, and concludes that these could be contained or responded to within the remit of appropriate duty of care if supported within an online context.

Face-to-face support as an adjunct to online interactions

There may also be instances where an online client requests, or is offered, the opportunity to meet face-to-face with a practitioner as an extension of the online relationship. This may occur within an organisational context or sole practitioner practice. Within the context of therapeutic online support, there are features such as transference and counter-transference which could influence the dynamics of the relationship and the potential for a positive outcome when making the transition into face-to-face interactions. In these and other professional contexts, it is important to consider the following points when assessing the benefits and disadvantages of offering such a resource to clients:

- Working online can promote a curiosity regarding features of each person within the online relationship. It would be inappropriate to encourage face-to-face encounters to satisfy such curiosity.
- In all circumstances, online clients should be informed prior to a face-to-face appointment that they will be meeting with the practitioner who facilitated the online interactions. It would be unacceptable for a client to arrive for a face-to-face meeting without this knowledge and their informed consent.
- Where a client initiates a request for a face-to-face meeting following a series of online interactions, the client should be provided with the option of meeting with a different practitioner. Clients should be supported with a referral to an alternative appropriate resource in circumstances where an additional practitioner cannot be resourced.
- Where a practitioner requests that a client attends for a face-to-face meeting, time should be allocated prior to this occurring where the purpose and potential dynamics of such a transition are discussed.

EXERCISE 6.3

CLIENT ASSESSMENT

- What features would be required within the assessment process in your particular sphere of practice when working online with clients?
- What distinct differences do these hold to other practitioner settings that you are familiar with? Explore the reasons behind specific requirements being a feature in your field of practice.
- What instances may lead you to undertake an ongoing assessment with clients and, where relevant, how would you approach the matter of onward referral?

Contracting

The term 'contracting' is highlighted within this context as a process that provides clarity and information during the initial stage of forming an online relationship with a client, whilst also establishing the responsibilities and adherence to service delivery by each party. In all areas of a practitioner's engagement with online clients, there is a necessity to introduce boundaries, which form the basis of a contract for the exchanges that will follow, including the issue of informed consent (Anthony and Goss, 2003). Such boundaries may include the frequency of exchanges available, number restrictions on word content in email exchanges, privacy and confidentiality issues, and so on. An example client agreement can be sourced from the companion website to this book. In addition to boundaries, there is a requirement for practitioners to provide information to clients which refer to their responsibilities as the professional delivering the service. The word 'contract' can seem formal and off-putting for some; it may therefore be preferable to title this as an 'online agreement' for work undertaken with clients. This can be posted on an online facility such as a website, with clients being directed towards reading and acknowledging the requirements of both parties.

The benefits of contracting to both practitioner and client are apparent, as this provides clarity on the nature of support and the practitioner's role and professional experience at the onset, in conjunction with expectations of the client.

The benefits of adopting the use of contracting with clients

The introduction of an online contract can assist with reducing the potential for misunderstandings and conflict to arise during the course of online exchanges, whilst also proving useful to refer back to if a source of conflict arises in relation to boundary issues.

The potential benefits of deciding to introduce contracting with clients fall into the following areas:

- Providing clearly defined boundaries on the limitations of service provided.
- Outlining any restrictions on the distribution of content from online exchanges by either party and the implications for breach of compliance.
- Identifying agreed alternative channels of communication that can be utilised in the event of technology or personal circumstances preventing contact through online exchanges.
- Providing a defined channel for addressing any misunderstandings or conflict which may arise in the course of online exchanges. In instances where conflict or misunderstandings cannot be resolved, providing guidance on procedures to follow where external mediation or grievance resolution is sought.
- Stipulating the jurisdictional restrictions regarding the hearing of any complaints or grievances arising from the content of online exchanges.
- Clarification regarding appointment arrangements and payment (where applicable).

EXERCISE 6.4

CLIENT CONTRACTS

- Consider your initial feelings and response in requesting clients to negotiate and agree to an online contract prior to proceeding with online exchanges.
- What do you consider to be the potential advantages and disadvantages of using contracting with clients in your field of professional online practice?
- Consider what would constitute essential elements of a client contract within the context of your professional practice.

Online risk assessment

As clients are physically distanced from the practitioner and organisations supporting professionals who work online, there is a reduced opportunity to manage instances where clients present in a manner which indicates they are at risk of harm to themselves or others. This therefore presents practitioners and organisations with a requirement to consider how such occurrences can be effectively responded to and managed.

In a face-to-face context, there is the obvious advantage of gaining visual and auditory indicators which highlight where a client may be entering a phase of instability. When conducting an online practice, the practitioner is reliant on the client to provide indications of this during an online exchange, in conjunction with drawing upon their attunement with the client and online counselling skill expertise to determine where a process of risk assessment is required. In a therapeutic context, many counselling services and mental health services utilise a risk assessment model at the point of a client entering into the service, and can draw from the results of this to assess the level of risk at varying points of the therapeutic relationship. An example of such a tool is the CORE System (Clinical Outcomes for Routine Evaluation), which has been designed and widely used in the UK within counselling, psychotherapy, and other psychological therapy services (available at www.coreims.co.uk).

CORE provides the opportunity for client and practitioner to determine risk in the pre-therapy stage and throughout the course of a contract, whilst also being utilised as a tool for measuring clinical outcomes. Where services decide not to adopt assessment resources, the practitioner could be left with the responsibility of forming a professional decision on how they can engage the client in discussing the matter, in conjunction with seeking support from their clinical supervisor and any additional resources available.

Chapter 4 refers to the potential for a process of online disinhibition to occur when using CMC. This may therefore increase the likelihood of clients revealing circumstances where they are experiencing risk to themselves or others. Overall, it is beneficial for the practitioner to have considered how disclosure by a client, or indications that the client or others may be at risk, is to be included and managed within their online service delivery.

Although more unlikely, such instances may arise where the nature of online communication is not related to therapeutic practice. This may also be evident in circumstances where a client does not have access to professionals or other personal networks that can assist with providing emotional support. It is therefore pertinent that practitioners in all areas of online practice consider how they would respond to such a disclosure based upon the level of responsibility they hold for duty of care and onward referral to appropriate support. A simulated example is give in Box 6.2.

Box 6.2   Risk assessment and duty of care

Dave is a qualified and experienced life coach who is developing a successful online practice. He is working with an online client called Mathew who requested support with his interpersonal skills which are a strong feature within his work role as a customer service manager. During the fourth online exchange, Mathew discloses that he has recently separated from his partner of four years and is struggling with the emotional response to this. He indicates that he has experienced a previous period of suicidal ideation during the breakdown of his first long-term relationship, whilst also mentioning that he fears the same reaction to the current circumstances. Mathew also discloses that he did not seek support during the first occurrence and felt more at ease to broach the subject through the current online communication, in conjunction with the strength of the relationship he felt was developing with Dave.

Dave is not qualified as a counsellor and has no previous experience of supporting clients who are potentially moving into risk of harm to self. He initially feels uncertain how to react to Mathew's emotional statements, but responds by offering an empathic and supportive reply where he outlines his lack of experience and knowledge with clients who indicate they may be at risk of harm, whilst also recommending to Mathew that he seek assistance from his GP as a resource of medical support. Dave suggests that Mathew may want to consider some face-to-face counselling, highlighting that as Mathew had taken the first step in revealing his feelings online, he may now feel more comfortable in considering the benefits of discussing this further with a face-to-face practitioner who would be better placed to support Mathew if his emotional well-being deteriorated further.

Mathew agrees to Dave's suggestions, and during the process of securing the recommended additional support, they agree to maintain contact. Once this is in place, they reach a mutual agreement that Mathew should temporarily cease the life coaching sessions and resume them at a point where he is feeling that his emotional state is settled and he is able to focus on his initial goals for their work together.

EXERCISE 6.5

MANAGING RISK OF SELF-HARM OCCURRENCES

If you are intending to adopt the use of online counselling skills within a sphere of practice which is outside of the remit relating to supporting clients who present at risk of self-harm, consider how you might respond to circumstances such as those identified in Box 6.2. What specific systems will you need to have in place to support clients and yourself in the event of such instances occurring?

Confidentiality

In the general context of communicating and adopting the use of counselling skills with clients in an online setting, the subject of confidentiality raises a variety of considerations and is influenced by the sphere in which the professional conducts their practice. In a therapeutic context, client confidentiality is paramount to compliance with ethical requirements, and breaches of appropriate conduct can lead to disciplinary action and suspension of membership or accreditation. For those practitioners whose work is conducted within support or guidance occupational fields, there will be directives which indicate the level of confidentiality appropriate to client work. In all instances, it is important to consider how the process of maintaining the required level of confidentiality can be achieved when adopting an online practice, whilst also providing clarity to clients regarding the boundaries of confidentiality which can be assured. Where conducting online communication with clients is a new venture for practitioners, it is beneficial to seek support from professionals who can assist with developing and maintaining systems which meet the identified requirements for client confidentiality, security of personal data, and content of sessions or online meetings.

The subject of confidentiality within an online practice would generally fall within the following areas, which will be discussed in detail below:

- confidentiality of client data
- confidentiality of material relating to online exchanges
- sharing of client information and the content of online exchanges with other professional colleagues: case discussion meetings, onward referral, supervision of client work.

Confidentiality of client data

The legal issues relating to the use and storage of client material are discussed in detail within Chapter 1, pages 26–27.

Confidentiality of material relating to online exchanges

A distinct benefit to practitioners and clients when working with CMC lies in the potential for both parties to have a complete record of any exchanges which have occurred. This can be particularly helpful where either person wishes to look back over the content for a variety of purposes, including any or all of the following:

- Referring back to a discussion topic.
- Clarifying any misunderstandings.
- Presenting material for the purpose of clinical or general supervision activities.
- In a therapeutic context, clients have the benefit of a full copy of their therapeutic process.
- In the unfortunate circumstances where a complaint is made against either party, a full account can be presented in the process of substantiating a grievance.

In conjunction with the potential benefits of having a full record of online exchanges, there is a requirement to consider how such comprehensive data and personal details can be protected against breaches of confidentiality. There will be distinct differences in how this is approached within the many facets of online services available to clients. An overriding consideration is the importance of complying with legal requirements relating to the holding and storage of such data, and briefing all staff on such requirements where involved in the administration of services.

Sharing of client information and the content of online exchanges with other professional colleagues: case discussion meetings, onward referral, supervision of client work

Variations in the sharing of client data and communication content will be governed by the context of the practitioner's professional practice. Such variations will influence the manner in which material generated from online exchanges can be shared with others outside of the online relationship. Where professional guidelines and contracts agreed with clients include the sharing of information and material generated from online exchanges, it is relevant to consider how such material will be disseminated. This could involve printing off material in a written format and forwarding on, or mailing electronically to a recipient. In either case, it is pertinent to remember that there is an increased likelihood of the notes containing more personally revealing information than is evident in more traditional forms of practitioner and client communication. An example of this would arise if using synchronous communication with a client and the practitioner has identified the client in a contacts list under their actual name. In the setting where emails are used in client work, it would be likely that the header of the message has the client's name and email account listed in conjunction with other personally identifiable material. One could argue that traditional forms of communication would hold similar potential for holding revealing data and therefore the risk of breaching confidentiality would not be increased in the context of online interactions. A distinct difference within the context of sending client data electronically to other recipients is that this medium may have an increased chance of being intercepted by unauthorised persons, or may be viewed by others where the recipient is not mindful of maintaining privacy of their Internet activity. It is therefore strongly advised to check all content of material sent for dissemination, and remove data which could compromise the boundaries of confidentiality agreed with clients. This process would also apply when storing either hard or electronic copies of client material. Where actual client material has been distributed for the purpose of clinical supervision, it is pertinent to request that hard and electronic copies are appropriately destroyed or deleted after the intended purpose has been executed. In all contexts, clients should be provided with information at the onset which details the incidences where either their personal data or information from online exchanges may be distributed or shared with others.

It is noted that some services do not keep records of online exchanges and have consciously adopted this practice as a specific policy within their organisational procedures.

⒠⒲⒠⒭⒞⒤⒮⒠   ⒍.⒍

CONFIDENTIALITY PROCEDURES

Compile a list of the specific procedures required within your area of professional practice which relate to confidentiality issues and the sharing or dissemination of data generated from client exchanges. Consider what systems are required to ensure appropriate management of such systems within the context of online exchanges.

Endings

There are a number of variations in the potential endings which a practitioner may encounter when working online with clients. This is influenced by the duration and nature of the online relationship encountered, and also apparent variation in scope within the framework of a service delivery. Endings are also influenced by variations in CMC facilities adopted for client interactions. In the context of contracted sessions with an agreed ending, there will be the factor of asynchronous and synchronous communication, which generates a difference in how they might be experienced. Within asynchronous working, the ending will not be experienced in 'real time' and will be planned and considered during the period of final exchanges between practitioner and client. In the context of synchronous exchanges, the ending will preferably have been discussed and occur where both parties are engaged in real-time communication. This can affect the impact of the ending for both client and practitioner, as in asynchronous interaction, both parties will not be in the 'online company' of the other as they draw the interaction or relationship to a close. There are distinct benefits for the practitioner to send the final email within the closing down or ending of the online communication in order to avoid the potential for a client to introduce new material within their final email which cannot be responded to by the practitioner. Within a synchronous ending, both parties have the simultaneous opportunity to contribute to the ending.

This section focuses on the most commonly experienced endings with clients and endeavours to include relevance to the multitude of perspectives where online endings, alongside the use of online counselling skills, will be included in a practitioner's professional practice. The endings discussed hold similarity to those encountered within face-to-face interactions, but require more explicit discussion within online work due to the absence of a physical presence during the process.

A single online interaction

The context of a practitioner providing a single online interaction to their client base may fall within a therapeutic, mental health, educational, welfare setting, or other background. There will be specific requirements, either organisational or professional, which influence aspects of how an appropriate ending will be conducted by a practitioner. Further to this, there are prerequisite elements which form an appropriate online ending to a one-off or single interaction. These fall into the following areas:

1. The client is notified at the beginning of the interaction that the session will include time for an ending to take place.
2. An appropriate proportion of the session time is allocated to provide a suitable ending (for a one-hour meeting, this would be 5–10 minutes, dependent on the nature of the interaction).
3. The ending time is shared appropriately for both parties to contribute, and is relevant to the apparent needs of both client and practitioner. The practitioner should ask a client if they have anything to say which is outstanding from their initial intent for the session, or from anything which has arisen during the course of the interaction.
4. A summary of the interaction and clarification of any outstanding points should be provided by the practitioner, particularly if action is required by either party following discussion points within the meeting.
5. An appropriate 'sign-off' should be offered by the practitioner, just as would occur in a face-to-face interaction.

An ongoing therapeutic relationship

In instances where a client and practitioner have been engaged in an ongoing online therapeutic relationship, the ending of the online interaction will hold many representations for both parties. The significance of an ending will necessitate appropriate consideration from a practitioner in order for this to form a positive element of the online relationship. Just as occurs within face-to-face interactions, the closing of an online therapeutic relationship holds great significance, and therefore online endings should also be given due consideration. If we assume that the ending has been mutually agreed by both parties, the key points that will influence a positive conclusion are:

1. Where a contracted number of sessions have been agreed with a client, the ending date is held in mind by the practitioner, and at appropriate intervals invites discussion with the client regarding the date and ending of the online relationship.

2. If it becomes apparent that the original contracted number of sessions has been over-estimated, or the client is stating that they do not require the initial agreed number, then an explicit ending should be agreed that provides an opportunity for outcomes of the therapeutic intervention to be discussed. The practitioner may also feel it relevant to offer the option for the client to return in the future if further assistance is required. If the medium itself has impacted upon the client choosing to end, the practitioner should offer support to the client in securing further support in a more suitable format. There may be occasions where both client and practitioner feel that referral to another online practitioner who holds specialism in an area which has not been accommodated within the existing provision would be relevant.

3. As within face-to-face therapeutic endings, a client may request something specific to be included within a final session as a personal representation of concluding in a manner which is beneficial. Both practitioner and client may need to discuss this within the sessions prior to ending in order to determine how this can be achieved in an online context with the absence of physical and verbal expression.

4. Online closure can be experienced in a different manner to that which is encountered in face-to-face interactions, due to the ending being represented by selecting 'send' to an email or the closing of an online synchronous discussion. This is very different to a client standing up, collecting their personal items, saying 'goodbye', and walking out of the counselling room door. During a synchronous conclusion, the ending could be experienced by a momentary sense of conveying a textual farewell expression which is 'held' somewhere in cyberspace and then closed. In an asynchronous context, the ending is secured by selecting the 'send' button to a final email, and in the case of a practitioner, not knowing how it has been received by a client unless read-receipts are requested within the initial contracting stages. Each person within the online relationship experiences their part of the ending physically alone. In circumstances where a final exchange occurs through asynchronous contact, it is advisable to request a read-receipt to ensure that the client has received the communication.

An ongoing supportive relationship

The nature of endings within an ongoing supportive relationship will vary according to the contextual setting of the organisation providing the support and the remit of the online practitioner or service provided. There is likely to be a vast range of professional circumstances where online support is provided. The aim of these guidelines is to provide generic aspects of endings which will require consideration by practitioners working in this field of work.

In the forming of an online continuing supportive relationship, there is the likelihood of a professional emotional bond forming between the client and practitioner, and as such this will have an impact on how each will contribute and experience the ending of the relationship. All the points highlighted in the previous discussion relating to endings within a therapeutic relationship will apply, but will be encountered as distinct to the professional conduct and requirements of the specialist support area of each practitioner who reads this book.

Where a supportive relationship includes the practitioner imparting information, advice, and referral to other agencies, this will form a strong relevance to ensuring that all necessary arrangements and information have been clearly communicated to clients prior to ending the relationship. Where a client is expected to follow up information or resources which have been identified within an online supportive relationship, explicit guidance should be communicated and a client's understanding of this should be checked, due to a reduced ability to confirm understanding through the absence of physical and auditory confirmation.

A significant benefit of online communication and endings lies in the fact that most online services provide the opportunity for a client to retain the content of sessions making them available to read through at a later point. In the context of endings, an online client can go back and read through the content of a final interaction at will, and as such this can assist in securing a beneficial sense of closure (Murphy and Mitchell, 1998).

Session endings due to technology failure

Where practitioners use computer-mediated technology as a tool for communication and establishing helping relationships, they will experience instances where:

- contact with clients is hindered or prevented by technology and equipment failure; and
- meeting online with a client is not possible due to difficulties being experienced by either party, or at times an abrupt ending will occur due to technical faults or difficulties arising during the course of an interaction.

This can feel very disconcerting and frustrating for both practitioner and client, particularly if the ending occurs during an important thread of discussion. It is important to take the precaution of having an alternative method of communicating with a client in the event of a technology issue which cannot be quickly resolved. This may include having exchanged telephone numbers for use in the event of such circumstances. The client may also be willing to continue with face-to-face meetings until the problem is resolved, if practically possible for both parties. During the initial opening dialogue of an online interaction or contracting phase of an online relationship, it is advisable to clarify how contact can be maintained during a technology breakdown in order to avoid undue distress if this occurs. Box 6.3 gives an example of technology issues preventing a pre-arranged online appointment.

Box 6.3*   Sam experiences a technology breakdown

Julie has arranged a second synchronous online meeting with Sam, as both parties had agreed that supplementing asynchronous contact with asynchronous meetings was proving beneficial to the level of relational engagement and the overall quality of the online relationship. Just prior to the scheduled meeting, Julie receives an email from Sam who is experiencing difficulties with a consistent online connection due to a power failure in her village.

Julie replies by email suggesting three alternatives to Sam: the first option is to postpone the meeting and re-schedule at a convenient time for both parties; the second option is to continue with the arranged meeting and if they experience a loss in connection, to continue by telephone; the third option is to arrange an email exchange the following day. Fortunately, at the time of Julie sending her email to the client, Sam was not experiencing a further power failure.

Sam replies to Julie by telephone, as they had exchanged telephone numbers at the onset of the counselling contract and agreed this as an alternative communication route in the event of technology issues preventing contact through CMC. Sam explains that she is currently experiencing a further power failure and would prefer to arrange an appointment for the following day. Sam confirms that there are no urgent issues which she was hoping to address within the session and they agree a time for a synchronous meeting, with the option of conducting a telephone session if the power failure issues persist.

EXERCISE   6.7

DEALING WITH
TECHNOLOGY BREAKDOWN

Consider how you might approach the circumstances identified within Box 6.3. What might have been the potential implications of Julie seeking to maintain contact with Sam via email contact, and not telephoning the client as an initial response to the circumstances of the power failure?

What other options might Julie have been able to suggest to Sam during the subsequent telephone conversation that would comply with professional and ethical directions for ensuring appropriate support to online clients?

Summary

The subject of assessment, contracting, and confidentiality when engaging with clients in online exchanges raises many considerations which are generic across the range of services available in this field of practice. This extends further into specific contexts where the practitioner is employing the use of online counselling skills with clients. The content of this chapter has detailed features that provide a basis for thought on the individual practitioner and organisation's relevance to include such processes within their professional activities. The relevance of relating all subject matter covered to individual practice will obviously be influenced by the nature of service delivery where the practitioner is employed. That being noted, it is pertinent to acknowledge that there are distinct benefits in adopting an assessment and contracting process, including the clarity it offers for both the professional and clients on the boundaries of service provision and agreed channels for addressing technology issues and any resulting misunderstandings, conflict, or breach of legal requirements which may arise during the course of the online relationship.

Points for consideration

- How do you envisage that assessment and contracting would advantage or hinder the effectiveness of your online exchanges with clients?
- How might you present the process of assessment and contracting to clients in order for this to provide a positive element to the online relationship?
- Having considered the relevance of assessment and contracting within the context of your professional framework, what do you regard as the overall advantage to yourself, clients, and organisation in adopting the use of, or revising, current assessment and contracting processes to comply with appropriate online practice?

References

Anthony, K. and Goss, S. (2003) *Technology in Counselling and Psychotherapy: A Practitioner's Guide*. London: Sage.

Anthony, K. and Jamieson, A. (2005) *Guidelines for Online Counselling and Psychotherapy*, 2nd edition. Lutterworth: British Association for Psychotherapy. p. 4.

Kraus, R., Zack, J. and Stricker, G. (2004) *Online Counselling: A Handbook For Mental Health Professionals*. San Diego, CA: Elsevier/Academic Press. pp. 80, 231.

Madahar, L. (2004) *Managing e-Guidance Interventions within HE Careers Services: A New Approach to Providing Guidance at a Distance*. Manchester: HESCU.

Murphy, L. and Mitchell, D. (1998) 'When writing helps to heal: email as therapy', *British Journal of Guidance & Counselling*, 26 (1): 21–32.

Pergament, D. (1998) 'Internet psychology: current status and future regulation', *Health Matrix: Journal of Law Medicine*, 8 (2): 233–79.

Suler, J. and Fenichel, M. (2000) *Assessing a Person's Suitability for Online Therapy: Clinical Case Study Group Findings*. International Society for Mental Health Online. Available at www.ismho.org/builder//?p=page&id=222.

Further reading, references, resources, and skill development activities relating to the subject matter within this chapter can be sourced via the companion website to this book.

PROFESSIONAL CONSIDERATIONS IN ONLINE PRACTICE

Online counselling skill topics presented in this chapter:

- Maintaining appropriate boundaries with clients within online inter-actions and online communities
- Appointment schedules and organising an appropriate working envi-ronment for online practice
- Online practitioner professional responsibilities
- The place of professional creativity and encompassing differing the-oretical perspectives when seeking to engage online with clients

Exercises and vignettes are included within this chapter, demonstrating the skills in practice and encouraging thought on the subject matter discussed.

The purpose of this chapter is to outline the appropriate recommendations for organising an online practice in a manner which complies with the ethical and legal guidelines appropriate to a practitioner application of online counselling and guidance skills. Such recommendations are beneficial to both practitioner and client and provide a framework of professional and ethical online practice. There are specific features within the development and management of such a work schedule which require consideration as they hold distinct variations to those encountered within a face-to-face context. Such elements are presented within this chapter and highlighted in a manner which encourages the reader to consider how they can be applied to their intended or current online practice.

There will be two main distinct variations within the work schedules and facets of service delivery for readers of this book:

- Practitioners who work from home or an office using computer-mediated technology to communicate with clients.
- Organisations who deploy online practitioners to deliver a service via a computer-mediated system.

The contents of this chapter include relevance to both variations.

Maintaining appropriate boundaries with clients within online interactions and online communities

The subject of appropriate boundary containment within online practice has featured as an interwoven topic throughout the book. Within this section, I focus on considerations which those who are new to engaging with others online may find beneficial, by highlighting the potential to overlook how having an online identity and presence needs additional thought on the impact of online boundary issues. This applies both in engagements with individual clients and within online community groups.

Boundaries are an essential feature within all spheres of professional practice and remain so when engaged in working online with clients. Within therapeutic practice, ethical and legal stipulations provide a guide for the face-to-face practitioner in maintaining appropriate boundaries with clients. Many of these directives transfer across naturally to this context of working, whilst additional considerations are required due to the variety of technology resources utilised to deliver a service to clients.

Contact from clients, or 'bumping into' clients outside of contracted session boundary times

An example of a distinction between face-to-face and online working can be illustrated by considering the difference between online communities in comparison to a physically located community. An individual may have a 'presence' or inhabit many online meeting places, and no doubt will have many contacts listed within their email accounts, Internet chat, instant messaging facilities, Skype contacts, mobile phone or Internet texting facility, and so on. When opening up a connection to the Internet, an individual's PC will often automatically connect them to any such facilities they have installed and remain active on their computer. This process can alert others to the fact that the person is 'online' and potentially available to engage with. This could be equated to an individual initiating an 'open house' for invited or uninvited visitors to knock on the door and request entry. As there is the potential for increased awareness of others being active online, this may highlight that a practitioner could be contactable or available when engaged in a client appointment, or outside of contractual appointment times, particularly where personal email accounts or other online communication contact details have been shared with others during the course of client work. Such considerations are also relevant within online supervision arrangements, and clear boundaries should be agreed during the scheduling of appropriate contact with a supervisor (Anthony and Jamieson, 2005).

Where both practitioner and clients inhabit online chat rooms or forums, and so on, there is also the likelihood that they may accidentally bump into each other through an undisclosed mutual interest. Circumstances such as this can be avoided by practitioners ensuring that their professional and personal online communication accounts are distinct, and where indications of boundary issues become apparent through online associations, take appropriate action to withdraw from situations which could compromise client boundaries. A feature that many individuals using the Internet both enjoy and take advantage of is the use of avatars, which can disguise actual identity to others. This could therefore lead to both practitioner and client 'meeting' with each other accidentally online, and holds the potential for neither party to realise this unless recognising each other through communication style or narrative content. Situations like this would not occur in the same manner when working face-to-face with clients, and where they do arise, have the scope to be addressed promptly. These points are particularly relevant to online therapeutic practice where boundaries are considered paramount to conducting professional duties. This factor therefore requires thought regarding necessary steps to reduce the likelihood of any negligence on a practitioner's part increasing the possibility for such situations to occur. Consideration should also be given to circumstances where a practitioner's clients may bump into each other online, and the potential implications of such circumstances.

Contact initiated by clients outside of contracted boundary limits

It is usual practice within professional face-to-face client and practitioner relationships that communication outside of the contracted session or meeting would be limited, and used for emergencies or for cancelling appointments. In situations where contact is sought by a client outside of a session time, there is the opportunity for a practitioner to limit the volume of dialogue and respond synchronously to clients. In the context of computer-mediated communication (CMC), clients may contact practitioners by email or other sources out of office hours. In such situations, the practitioner does not hold the same potential to manage the communication and content received, or to reply synchronously. It is therefore appropriate to consider what personal boundaries and limitations would need to be in place in order to appropriately manage and respond to such occurrences.

Where practitioners are conducting appointments through an email system, it is relevant to include information for clients during the onset of a working agreement, which clarifies the time constraints in being able to respond to both scheduled and unscheduled contact from clients. This provides clarity for both parties and prevents the potential for blurring of boundaries and maintaining an organised appointment schedule.

There are distinct benefits to managing an online practice via a website, as it can serve as a 'screen' which places a practitioner one step removed from direct availability to contact from clients. This is helpful in avoiding circumstances such as those previously identified, as the online practitioner will be utilising generic email addresses, synchronous chat facilities, and so on, which are integral to the website, as opposed to personal accounts.

Where such a system has been adopted, clients should be provided with information relating to anticipated response times in the event of seeking contact, either prior to engaging with a practitioner or during the course of contracted online meetings (NBCC, 2007).

Box 7.1*   Sam encounters boundary issues

The practitioner, Julie, receives an unexpected email from her client, Sam. They had initially contracted for weekly exchanges, which had developed during the course of the online relationship to include both asynchronous and synchronous meetings. Julie's 'turnaround' time for replies to Sam's emails had been agreed as 24 hours from the time of receiving correspondence from Sam.

In an unscheduled email, Sam conveys a sense of urgency in requiring a response from Julie as she had been engaged in an argument with her adolescent daughter, which resulted in the daughter walking out of the family home and not returning at the agreed evening curfew time. Sam explains that her daughter returned home the next day and refused to discuss where she had spent the previous night. Sam was obviously very distraught when writing the email, and indicates that she does not have alternative means of emotional support at hand besides Julie to discuss the previous evening's events.

During the course of all exchanges, Sam has been mindful of boundaries agreed with Julie and has not requested support in addition to scheduled meetings or exchanges. Following the unscheduled communication described in Box 7.1, Julie decides that under the duty of care she applies to her client work, it is appropriate to send an initial brief reply to Sam indicating she has received the email and can hear how upset Sam is by the previous evening's events. Julie explains that she is engaged with other scheduled work until later in the day, but confirms that she will send a full reply to Sam by early evening, whilst requesting for Sam to reply with an indication of any adverse impact on her well-being if required to wait for a full response. Julie also offers the option of a telephone appointment if preferred by the client. Sam replies, stating that she is agreeable to waiting until later that day for support and would prefer email contact. The further action taken by Julie is outlined in Box 7.2.

Box 7.2*   Action taken by Julie

As Julie may not be available to offer such a speedy reply to the client in the future, she makes a conscious note to reiterate this in her email reply regarding the scope of flexibility within her schedule to respond spontaneously, whilst also encouraging a dialogue with Sam regarding options of additional local support the client may be able to secure if similar circumstances arise in the course of their online contract (NBCC, 2007).

Julie decides to review her current systems for conveying availability to clients at the onset of contracting to ensure that she is accommodating potential emergency situations in accordance with ethical guidelines and potential client needs.

EXERCISE   7.1

ONLINE BOUNDARY ISSUES

Consider what might present as potential boundary issues within your sphere of professional online practice. How might these be approached in the process of developing an ethical framework for service delivery?

Appointment schedules and organising an appropriate working environment for online practice

Organising and managing an online appointment schedule requires skill and a realistic view of what period of time is conducive to maintaining a healthy balance when administering professional practice through the use of computer-mediated technology. To assist in the planning of appointment schedules, it is relevant to consider the environment and actual location where an online practice is conducted. A distinct difference when working online in comparison to supporting clients in a physical location is the reliance on Internet systems, technology, and equipment to support the delivery of effective practice. Face-to-face client practice provides a certain level of security and reassurance by the physical locality adopted for work activities being stable, with practitioners unlikely to encounter incidents where client appointments are disrupted due to structural building faults. When reliant on computer-mediated technology, this is not the case, and situations may arise where client appointments cannot be fulfilled. With the likelihood that problems will be experienced at some point which impact on the ability to deliver or fulfil a client appointment, it is relevant to consider how this could affect appointment schedules and to take precautionary steps to minimise the potential impact upon service delivery. Clients should be informed at the onset of procedures in the event of such occurrences.

The following points highlight variations within online and face-to-face work schedules and offer suggestions to assist with developing appropriate facilities for appointments and location resources for an online practice:

- An online practice would usually necessitate being located at a PC for the duration of client appointments. Therefore, it is advisable to consider the reasonable limitations in the context of consistent periods of time to be engaged in online practice, which are also favourable within a healthy work routine, and plan appointment schedules accordingly.
- Where an online practitioner is providing non-appointment-based contact with clients, and therefore offers the equivalent of a 'drop in' service, it is important to consider the implications for clients who are potentially 'queuing' outside the practitioners 'online practice door' for a synchronous appointment. In the case of email, or asynchronous contact with clients, practitioners should acknowledge receipt of client communication and reply with details which indicate when they will form and send a full response.
- Where appointment-based interactions with clients are a feature within an online practice, adopted systems should allow sufficient time to accommodate re-scheduling in the event of a technology issue preventing a session being completed to its full duration. It is also advisable to have discussed and agreed with clients how disrupted sessions can be continued using alternative means of communication.
- Where a combination of activities is evident within work schedules, such as being engaged in both face-to-face interactions and online appointments, it is pertinent to consider how the two can work in harmony and not adversely impact upon each other. To illustrate this point further, consider the practical resources which are required for both activities and consider how these can be accommodated within the locality of your work area.

Box 7.3 gives an example relating to appropriate boundaries in online communication with clients.

Box 7.3 Managing contacts when engaged online

Marion is employed as an online counsellor who works from home using her own computer and Internet connection. She accesses her client schedules and sessions through a provider's website. She frequently uses Skype as an online communication resource as it provides the opportunity to converse with colleagues, family, and friends without the expense of phone charges. She has many people listed within her Skype contacts directory and receives frequent calls from others during the course of her working day. When engaged in client appointments, Marion always ensures that Skype and all other online communication resources installed on her PC are temporarily disabled in order to avoid any of the people from her contact list trying to initiate communication with her during the time she is engaged with client work. Marion considers this to equate to the same practice as placing 'engaged' on a counselling room door when holding a session with a face-to-face client, and therefore prevents any unnecessary distractions or disruptions during her client appointments.

EXERCISE 7.2

Consider both the personal and professional advantages and disadvantages in delivering an online client service using:

- an appointment-based system; and
- the equivalent of a face-to-face 'drop in' appointment system.

Online practitioner professional responsibilities

This section discusses the considerations that are pertinent to delivering an online practice where appropriate professional responsibilities are defined and adopted to ensure that service delivery meets required standards, appropriate accessibility, and positive outcomes. Many of these features hold a similarity to those considered by face-to-face practitioners but require additional thought when engaging with clients online.

Working online and encompassing diversity and related factors which may impact upon an online relationship

It is not my intention within this section to define diversity and inclusiveness. Attempting such an illustration within the confines of this book would not be achievable. Specific references to material which discusses this subject can be found within the companion website to this book. What I would like to present to readers, and encourage professional consideration towards, is the likelihood of this subject being particularly relevant within online service delivery to clients.

Delivering an online practice provides the opportunity for practitioners to work across a global canvas and greatly increases the potential for encountering clients from a broader spectrum of diversity than would be available to an individual or service whose clients are sourced from within one physical location. This undoubtedly generates an increase in the diversity of issues presented by clients, in conjunction with variances in how such issues are communicated and expressed. From a client perspective, it also holds the potential to meet a practitioner who has a differing communication style and narrative emphasis to that which they are familiar.

The facility of a global customer market, accessible through the World Wide Web, has brought a further layer of significance to the subject of diversity to that which was evident prior to the advent of the Internet as a tool for global connectivity. The subject and relevance of global diversity is widely recognised and is the subject of discussion in all facets of society. Within this context, it is important to consider when engaging online with clients that culture does influence and affect communication, personal values, perceptions, values and behaviour, and so on. A client may present for online support without being requested to provide any form of identification or personal introduction. In such cases, both parties will begin to experience any apparent cultural and personal differences during the process of establishing an online relationship. This factor therefore places a level of responsibility on individuals and organisations who offer an online service to consider how they will accommodate a potential broad range of diversity within their online provision, whilst consciously seeking to overcome any apparent communication issues that arise with clients and inhibit the scope for a positive outcome.

The following points are key features in the process of enhancing communication and understanding diversity issues across a global platform:

- Considering and assessing the impact of personal communication style when interacting with a diverse spectrum of clients.
- Consciously working towards identifying and seeking a positive resolution in potential and actual communication gaps in the online interactions with clients, and inviting discussion with clients where it becomes apparent that there are differences in perceptions in helper–client relationships (Nelson-Jones, 2003).
- Seeking ways to assist clients where it becomes evident that they are experiencing difficulty in communicating their intended written narrative and dialogue.
- Proactively seeking to enhance skills which can assist in the process of communicating more effectively with language and cultural difference.
- Maintaining a commitment to self-exploration in areas where personal beliefs/stereotyping create barriers to interacting with positivity and congruence, including where cultural or diversity issues become apparent in client work.
- Consciously endeavouring to understand and develop empathy regarding the impact of values and beliefs from diverse cultural contexts.

An example of communication difficulties within global cultural variation and difference is illustrated in Box 7.4.

Box 7.4 Cultural communication difficulties

John is based in the UK and has a website which offers relationship coun-selling to online clients. He is qualified and skilled as an online counsellor, but only recently commenced engaging with clients within a global context. He is providing online support to Liz, an American female currently residing in Japan. During the course of their third email exchange, she discusses at length experiencing a recent epiphany and as such has formulated a new perspective for approaching future relationships and her potential for con-tributing to successful partnerships. John is not familiar with the term 'epiphany', but believes it relates to a kind of divine manifestation. Liz has assumed that John would be familiar with the term and has not elaborated on its meaning.

When replying to Liz, John styles his response on an assumption in his interpretation of the term as he feels reluctant to check out the specific meaning with the client in case this may undermine his credibility. Liz is confused by John's response and begins to feel that he may not be able to support her due to his lack of empathy and misinterpretation of her having a strong faith belief. Fortunately, Liz feels able to seek clarification of the meaning within John's reply and the misunderstanding is resolved, although it leaves a level of distrust for Liz regarding John's overall poten-tial to assist her with a positive outcome for her online sessions in case of further potential misinterpretations.

ⒺⓍⒺⓇⒸⒾⓈⒺ ⑦.③

DEALING WITH CULTURAL DIFFERENCES

Consider how you approach and seek to establish effective communication within the face-to-face context of engaging with clients when encountering cultural and diversity differences. Take into account the variations which will be apparent in the medium of working online with clients, such as the absence of physical presence and expression, and identify how you would seek to achieve effective communication and outcomes.

Insurance

I have included reference to professional indemnity insurance within this section as a signpost for online practitioners to check with their current insurers if they are covered to work online with clients, and also the specific requirements that insurers stipulate for validation of such insurance policies in the event of seeking assistance with a claim. Although working online opens up the potential to engage with clients across a global platform, insurance and other restricting features such as licensing/registration in countries such as the USA restrict practitioners from having open access to practice without appropriate entitlement. Not all insurers who provide a service to face-to-face practitioners will extend cover to include online practice, or any apparent jurisdictional and legal features which apply within the physical location of the online practice. It is therefore recommended that this point is clarified with insurers prior to establishing an online service, and where relevant alternative cover should be sought to include this aspect of client work.

Insurers who do include online engagement with clients within practitioner cover will stipulate that secure encrypted chat rooms are deployed when conducting synchronous sessions with clients.

Verification of practitioner and online service identity and credentials

When a client enters a face-to-face service, they have the advantage of being able to form an assessment of the credibility and validity of the provision based upon factors such as:

- Being able to meet and converse with personnel, the manner in which the physical attributes of the service are resourced, displayed signs, awards indicating professional affiliation and recognition, and so on.
- When they enter a practitioner's office, there may be certificates and validation indicators which signify that the client is encountering a professional who has competence attained through both training, professional affiliation, and experience. Where these are not displayed, a client can ask to see original copies to ascertain the credibility of the practitioner.

Such factors contribute to providing reassurance to clients that they are likely to receive the required level of service, and where this is not apparent, they can then decide to seek out more suitable alternatives. When seeking online support, a client does not have access to the same visual and physical reassurances. It is essential that the online service and practitioners seek ways that offer reassurance to clients that they are engaging with a reputable and qualified service. Often the first point of contact will be through a web-based 'shop window' such as a website. Clients will be looking for evidence that the service and professionals are sufficiently competent and qualified to provide the service they are promoting and offer ways in which clients can verify the information displayed, where desired. Online practitioners can achieve this in a variety of ways:

- Submit hard copy qualification certificates to online directories that authenticate and publish the details on their website. This information is accessible to a global public and clients can access the information to verify the authenticity of a practitioner's credentials. Provide information or a hyperlink for clients to directories where you are listed.
- Affiliate yourself, and your service, to professional organisations specialising in your sphere of practice and that have an online interface where clients can access directories or registers which provide authenticating information of their members.
- If you or your organisation are accredited or registered with a professional body, provide details of this on your website, and so on. It is relevant to include hyperlinks which can take a client directly to such organisations and assist in checking authenticity of these claims. Displaying logos provided by training organisations upon completion of certified online counselling courses can also be useful in providing reassurances.
- Where you have written articles or other material which have been published and are available online, provide a hyperlink to them from your website.
- Some clients prefer to see a photographic image of the online practitioner included on the website, as opposed to working without a physical representation of the practitioner. This may serve to enhance credibility.
- Without doubt, the manner in which a website is presented will influence a client's preference in contacting one practitioner or online service in comparison to another, but of course this alone would not serve to authenticate the service.

There are many ways in which clients can gain increased reassurances regarding both an online resource and the professional(s) who provide a service using this medium. Where valid reassurances can be provided, this will assist in giving both credibility to online services in general whilst also assisting in promoting a positive image and reputation of online professionals and services. In light of the evident tendency from some members of the global public towards negativity in respect of online resources and their potential credibility, this is particularly relevant.

Amongst other reputable global organisations, Anthony and Jamieson (2005) have published guidelines for online counselling and psychotherapy. Such guidelines provide detailed procedures for those delivering resources in this field of practice. As a practitioner's online service delivery increases in its diversity and numbers, this necessitates the implementation of professional conduct to be highlighted and published according to the nature of professional activity. This will further ensure the credibility and standards of such resources. In the context of general face-to-face therapeutic practice, the planned introduction of regulation will standardise such services and require all practitioners to be listed if intending to offer a service to clients. This will assist in providing reassurances to service users and potential clients.

In other areas of online support, where such requirements will not be imposed, this may prove more difficult for clients to have additional reassurance of a practitioner's suitability, qualifications, and experience to deliver an online practice.

ⒺⓍⒺⓇⒸⒾⓈⒺ   ⑦.④

ETHICAL PRACTICE

How might professionals who engage with clients in your area of specialism seek to enhance their authenticity and credibility to potential online clients?

What professional guidelines or code of ethics are in place within your sphere of professional practice which relates to client work, both in a face-to-face and online context?

In cases where online guidelines are not currently available, what do you consider naturally transfers across from a face-to-face framework, and what additional considerations need to be identified to ensure appropriate practice?

The place of professional creativity and encompassing differing theoretical perspectives when seeking to engage online with clients

The advent of the Internet for supporting and communicating with clients has opened up new channels of delivering a broad range of professional activities alongside the scope to be creative in how such services are structured and delivered. It is not my intent here to define how differing theoretical approaches can be adapted to online working, or illustrate how differing disciplines of professional practice can be applied, but rather to encourage readers to consider how aspects of their existing face-to-face practice might fit or transfer to an online medium. An example of an adaptable resource is the use of genograms (McGoldrick et al., 1999). This can provide greater clarification of client backgrounds and also save time in explanations being required during online exchanges. There is strong evidence to suggest that professionals from differing theoretical orientations are looking into ways of applying theoretical principles to work with computer-mediated therapy (Adams, 1998; Pelling and Renard, 2000; Kasket, 2003).

Whilst not ignoring the potential political agenda which some may highlight when considering the rationale for the NHS developing and implementing computer-based cognitive behavioural therapy (cCBT) resources within the UK, it is relevant to note that one of the packages in use, 'Beating the Blues', has been quoted as achieving results which are comparative to face-to-face CBT interventions. Research indicates that cCBT can be more effective in reducing patient waiting lists (NICE, 2004). The National Institute for Clinical Excellence (NICE) currently recommends cCBT, and a further product called 'Fear Fighter', which was endorsed by NICE and adopted for supporting clients who experience phobias, anxiety, and panic attacks (NICE, 2006). These resources are computer-based and are supported by health-care providers who check patients' progress. Such resources can reduce the stigma of seeking face-to-face support, whilst also possessing the capability to provide a more convenient route of support for patients.

The US Surgeon General's report (1999) indicated that approximately two-thirds of US citizens who need mental health-care did not access or receive it, and cited stigma as the primary reason for this. This and other global indicators which highlight a resistance from individuals to seek support with mental health issues due to evident personal and more general barriers does necessitate a review of services which could be expanded to include online resources and encourage a more inclusive and inviting service for clients. Such positive affirmation may also encourage practitioners from all theoretical orientations to consider the benefits of offering an online service for clients. Such a progression would therefore increase the variation in resources and available modalities for clients to select from.

In their *2006/2007 Annual Report*, the Samaritans stated that 184,000 global email contacts were received from clients, being an increase of just over 12 per cent on the previous year (four times higher than the increase within face-to-face contact), which apart from communication by letter, was the highest increase area of contact from clients in 2006. The Samaritans also conducted a pilot in 2006 where they introduced a SMS text messaging service. The Samaritans were presented with a special acknowledgement at the eWell-being Awards in 2007 for 'making a difference' in social, economic, and environmental benefits of information and communication technologies. The apparent success of such ventures might therefore encourage other disciplines and professionals to consider how aspects of their practice and specialisms can be transferred to provide effective additional resources for online clients, whilst also positively promoting and assisting online services for clients.

This point is particularly relevant in areas of practice where it has been established that specific groups within society are less likely to approach face-to-face services. Potentially, the barriers preventing individuals seeking access could be overcome by the presence of an online resource which can fulfil the requirements of effective service delivery. Such innovative ventures are also being rewarded in the USA with the awarding of e-therapy grants to support the development of further computer-mediated resources for clients (Allen, 2007).

EXERCISE   7.5

TRADITIONAL SKILLS IN AN ONLINE PRACTICE

Consider what features, or additional aspects, of your face-to-face practice could be provided within an online service delivery.

Where you adopt the use of creative 'tools' within your face-to-face practice, consider how these might be transferable when working with clients through computer-mediated technology.

Summary

In addition to evident ethical and legal requirements, there are professional deliberations which influence the effectiveness of online service delivery and outcomes for clients. This chapter has highlighted how such features can be applied within the structure of both practitioner and organisational practice. Where individuals work independently or are employed by an establishment providing an online service to clients, they will be required to consider how their personal and professional online presence is structured and managed in a manner which does not compromise the proficiency and credibility of their profession. It could be argued that this is established practice within the remit of face-to-face professional conduct and therefore would automatically transfer and apply when delivering an online practice. I hope that this chapter has generated thought and awareness in how additional aspects arising through computer-mediated support necessitate continuing thought in the process of adhering to boundaried, appropriate professional conduct and practice. The nature of an online presence and service provision does place a distinct screen which can generate increased anxiety regarding the validity and intent of service providers. It is therefore vital that both practitioners and online services actively seek to provide credible professional information regarding themselves which can be verified by clients as required.

As in face-to-face supportive relationships, online practitioners will have at hand a theoretical and personally developed 'tool bag' of activities and exercises which can be drawn upon during the course of their client work. Engaging with clients through computer-mediated technology opens up the potential to be equally as creative with such resources. Careful contemplation is required prior to inclusion as there is limited potential for practitioners to respond to or contain the resulting impact this may hold, as the medium does not provide the scope for access to all the visual, verbal, and auditory indicators present in face-to-face interactions.

There is an opportunity for those engaged in particular advancements in online service delivery to provide a platform for individuals and organisations by sharing examples of good practice and encourage continuing development and creativity within this context of client work.

Points for consideration

- What existing platforms are available to practitioners and organisations to engage with the process of sharing good practice in online service delivery within your area of specialism, and how could these be further expanded or enhanced in the process of informing others and encouraging continuing development in this area?
- What face-to-face resources which you currently include within face-to-face client encounters can be adapted to online interactions?
- What professional responsibilities within your particular sphere of practice would require consideration prior to engaging with online clients?

References

Adams, M. (1998) 'On the experience and representation of space', *Journal of the Society for Existential Analysis*, 9 (1): 2–16.

Allen, J. (2007) *SAMHSA Awards 4E Therapy Grants*. Federal Law News, Archive for the Federal Law Category. Available at http://etherapylaw.com/?cat=6.

Anthony, K. and Jamieson, A. (2005) *Guidelines for Online Counselling and Psychotherapy*, 2nd edition. Lutterworth: BACP. pp. 4, 5.

Kasket, E. (2003) 'Online counselling', *Journal of the Society for Existential Analysis*, 14 (1): 60–74.

McGoldrick, M., Gerson, R. and Shellenberger, S. (1999) *Genograms: Assessment and Intervention*. New York: Norton.

NBCC (2007) *The Practice of Internet Counseling: Internet Counseling Relationship (3 and 6)*. Greensboro, NC; National Board for Certified Counsellors & Center for Credentialising and Education: Available at www.nbcc.org/webethics2.

Nelson-Jones, R. (2003) *Basic Counselling Skills: A Helper's Manual*. London: Sage. p. 101.

NICE (2004) *Computerised Cognitive Behaviour Therapy for Depression and Anxiety Update: A Systematic Review and Economic Evaluation.* Technology assessment report commissioned by the HTA Programme on behalf of NICE (The National Institute for Clinical Excellence). Computerised cognitive behaviour therapy for depression and anxiety update: a systematic review and economic evaluation. Available at www.nice.org.uk/nicemedia/pdf/CCBT_assessment_report_review.pdf.

NICE (2006) *Computerised Cognitive Behaviour Therapy for Depression and Anxiety (Review): Quick Reference Guide.* National Institute for Health and Clinical Excellence. Available at www.nice.org.uk/nicemedia/pdf/TA097quickrefguide.pdf.

Pelling, N. and Renard, D. (2000) 'Counselling via the Internet: can it be done well?', *Psychotherapy Review*, 2 (2): 68–71.

Samaritans (2006/2007) *Support through Innovation: Annual Report & Accounts.* Available at www.samaritans.org/PDF/SamaritansAnnualReport2007.pdf.

US Surgeon General (1999) *Mental Health: A Report of the Surgeon General.* Available at www.surgeongeneral.gov/library/reports.htm.

Further reading, references, resources, and skill development activities relating to the subject matter within this chapter can be sourced via the companion website to this book.

PROFESSIONAL GUIDELINES FOR ONLINE PRACTICE

Online counselling skill topics presented in this chapter:

- Ethical practice and guidelines when engaged in online practice
- Membership of professional organisations and peer support
- Supervision arrangements for online practitioners

Exercises and vignettes are included within this chapter, demonstrating the skills in practice and encouraging thought on the subject matter discussed.

The first section of this chapter draws together key points relevant to effective and ethical practice, providing readers with a reference point for the development and implementation of online counselling skills service delivery.

Section two of this chapter outlines the distinct benefits of seeking affiliation to professional organisations which offer specialised support and resources to online practitioners. This is particularly pertinent as working with clients using computer-mediated communication is still in its infancy in comparison to traditional forms of client service delivery. Practitioners are advised to consider the benefits of both sharing their experiences with fellow online professionals whilst also seeking affiliation with specialist organisations which offer guidelines and resources for this field of practice.

Supervision may not be a feature for all who read this book, and there may be variations dependent on the context of online practice. Within any new professional venture, it is beneficial to seek guidance and support from a practitioner or supervisor who has existing experience and confidence in the service delivery being developed. It is therefore pertinent to consider the benefits of securing supervision in all manner of professional variations which are evident for readers of this book.

Ethical practice and guidelines when engaged in online practice

This section is presented in the format of ethical guidance for those professionals who conduct communication with clients through an online medium.

The guidelines have been developed from an original online counselling mini guide first published in the 2007 *AUCC Journal*, written by Evans (2007). They are not intended to substitute or supersede any existing published material such as the BACP *Guidelines for Online Counselling and Psychotherapy* (Anthony and Jamieson, 2005), the ISMHO (Ainsworth et al., 2000) 'Suggested Principles for the Online Provision of Mental Health Services, version 3.11', the ACA *Code of Ethics* (2007), and other relevant professional guidelines applicable to the jurisdiction of online practitioners' professional activity.

The guidelines within this section are presented with the aim of complementing existing directions for professionals employed in this field of practice, whilst also offering a framework of ethical practice in professional contexts where consideration to defining appropriate online practice have not currently been defined. The guidelines contained within this chapter relate to asynchronous and synchronous online communication with clients, and include service delivery using resources such as forums, tutorials, discussion boards, distance learning programmes, one-to-one online coaching, online counselling, online supervision, information and guidance support, and additional further-reaching professional activities. It is pertinent with a potential global client marketplace to consider relevant guidelines within both the jurisdiction of the practitioner's locality and in conjunction with those relevant to their clients (NBCC, 2007b).

Competencies of practitioners who adopt the use of online counselling skills

Adopting the use of counselling skills in an online context necessitates specialist competencies and enhanced skill development in order to work professionally and successfully with clients electronically through text-based narrative. It is relevant to acknowledge that the following recommendations hold specific relevance to duty of care and appropriate professional conduct. Practitioners should be:

- proficient in IT skills, Internet technology issues, and possess sufficient knowledge in the administration and storage of electronic information and data to achieve service delivery that complies with ethical and legal requirements
- sufficiently competent in maintaining electronic records and client information to avoid the possibility of compromising confidentiality or security of data, applying appropriate deliberation relative to the setting of the online practice
- experienced and competent in the process of assessment and contracting across a diverse range of client presenting issues

- sufficiently competent to consider the implications of appropriate assessment procedures for engaging with clients when transferring counselling skills to computer-mediated services
- mindful of maintaining awareness of the potential for online communication and expression to bring certain dynamics into the relationship which require proficiency in responding to, in a manner which provides a sense of containment for clients whilst also facilitating a positive outcome

Online practitioner skills training

A practitioner who is considering entering into this field of work should seek out courses which offer guidance on the necessary practical skills whilst also providing direction regarding the ethical and practical administration requirements of an online service. It is the responsibility of training providers to ensure that their students are familiar with this context of practice and the potential benefits and drawbacks to themselves as potential practitioners and the clients they may engage with in their future practice (Guterman and Kirk, 1999; Trepal et al., 2007).

Globally, there are distinct variations in licensing laws for establishing an online practice. It is therefore advisable that practitioners seek out training providers and courses which offer appropriate direction in this area, with course material that is specifically directed towards any evident jurisdictional and legal requirements within the location of the professional's online practice.

Initial assessment and ongoing risk assessment are key features in this field of practice and require competencies which are gained through specialist training. It would be inappropriate for a practitioner to become established in online therapeutic or mental health practice without undergoing the appropriate skill development and training, and knowledge of clinical and professional responsibilities (ACA, 2007).

Conducting professional practice using online counselling skills

Adherence to effective communication and maintaining an awareness of prominent dynamics which present during the course of working with clients is key to successful outcomes. The absence of a physical presence within online exchanges reduces the potential for a practitioner in having access to indications or observations of a client's physical and emotional well-being, and as such necessitates close attention to the content, variations in a client's online presentation, and the potential implications relating to duty of care.

The nature of online practice places an emphasis on the practitioner to clarify and support clients with the aim of minimising the potential impact of the following circumstances:

- Misunderstandings or conflict which occurs throughout the application, assessment, contracting, ongoing stages, and conclusion of the online relationship. Guidelines regarding resolution of potential misunderstandings and conflict should be outlined within the initial contract (BACP, 2005).
- Paying attention to any apparent online disinhibition by a client which may influence disclosure, and hold the potential to impact upon the emotional stability of a client, the potential for a positive outcome of the online interaction, and the client's well-being.
- Incidences resulting in a loss of contact with the practitioner through equipment failure, or the inability to gain access to online communication resources, therefore preventing scheduled meetings or appointments taking place or being completed.
- Assisting with appropriate onward referral where necessary, and conveying information to clients with regard to additional, reliable support resources available through the Internet or face-to-face services. Where online guidance or support is not sufficient to provide a satisfactory outcome for clients, or an emergency situation arises that cannot be supported by the online practitioner, it is pertinent to acknowledge limitations and collaborate with clients in an onward referral. Locally based resources should be indicated wherever possible (NBBC, 2007).
- Supporting clients with appropriate and boundaried endings where an identified focus of work has been completed. Where additional follow-on resources are required, clients should be supported by the practitioner in securing suitable progression to further systems of support.

Careful consideration and planning should be given to introducing a system of service delivery where any evident negative impact of occurrences, such as those identified in this section, is minimised. All aspects of service delivery should comply with legal and jurisdictional codes of practice within the resident country of the practitioner, and wherever possible those relevant to clients' country of residence.

Box 8.1 provides an illustration relating to duty of care and referral within an online practice.

Box 8.1*   Duty of care and referral

Julie has been providing online support for Sam over a period of eight sessions. The client was originally referred to Julie via Sam's GP.

Sam initially presented to Julie's service with concerns regarding her adolescent daughter and the breakdown of her relationship with an ex-partner.

During the course of a synchronous exchange, the manner in which Sam 'presents' her written narrative and dialogue is distinctly different to that which Julie has witnessed in a previous live session. Julie senses a great deal of lethargy in the client. Sam also discloses concerns that she may be developing depression, and is worried that this may be affecting her ability to appropriately care for her children.

As the online practitioner does not have the facility to invite Sam to attend a face-to-face appointment to assess the potential vulnerability of her and the children, she strongly recommends that Sam visits the referring GP to discuss her emotional well-being, whilst also requesting that Sam informs her of the outcome. In addition, Julie encourages discussion regarding support networks which the client may draw upon from within her family and friendship group to assist Sam in both her self-care and childcare arrangements.

During the contracting stage of the relationship, Sam had consented to being contacted by telephone if required. Julie bears this in mind as an option to pursue with the client if the highlighted concerns remain during the course of the following online exchanges.

Requirements for effective online service delivery

Planning, delivery, and administration of an online practice   The global variations in the structure and delivery style of available online services are multi-faceted and it is not the intention here to define the specifics of an effective service delivery and adopted administration systems. Individual circumstances and resources will affect the format of each service and the manner in which it is structured. This being noted, there remain important underpinning factors which cut beneath the variations in licensing laws and legalities apparent in a global context.

There are several factors underpinning considerations for online service delivery which should be in place and conveyed to clients at the onset of service delivery:

- Guidance and information relating to the potential for misunderstandings to arise and systems available to address such incidents.
- Clear guidelines relating to access and use of the online service. Such information should highlight what the online service expects of them as clients of the service, including the subject of maintaining privacy of material generated in the course of their relationship with a practitioner. This can be made available in electronic booklet form or provided within the service provider's web pages prior to commencing online interactions with clients.

- The structure of the appointment system and any apparent flexibility within this. Clients should also be informed of procedures in the event of delayed, cancelled, or missed appointments.
- Clear guidelines regarding the limitations of confidentiality.
- Due to the physically distanced relationship, it is pertinent to provide information which is visible and provides reassurance of a credible and professional service. Such information must be accessible to potential clients through web-based communication, such as a service provider's website.
- Provision of details regarding maintaining contact with a practitioner in the event of a technology issue or other loss of contact. This is particularly relevant where a practitioner has stated that they would attempt to make contact with a client by telephone or alternative means in such circumstances (Halpern, 2007).
- Clear information regarding payment for appointments (where applicable)

In circumstances where a practitioner has to cancel pre-arranged appointments due to technology issues or ill health, and so on, it is strongly recommended that systems are in place, including:

- Clients being notified in advance of their appointment time.
- Appropriate consideration being given to adopting systems which alleviate anxiety experienced by clients who are anticipating a scheduled appointment and subsequently cannot be fulfilled.
- In circumstances where a continuing inability to deliver online appointments occurs, a suitable alternative provision should be offered to clients. Alternatives may include suggesting a referral to a face-to-face adjunct of the service, or referral to an alternative online practitioner during the absence of the designated practitioner.

Box 8.2 provides an illustration of client referral resulting from circumstances where the designated online practitioner experiences an extended period of ill health. The example highlights the importance of effective and consistent communication during a period of absence.

Box 8.2   Client onward referral

Yan is co-tutor for a university-accredited distance learning course. He communicates with his students through a variation of mediums including Skype, email, and synchronous meetings using a secure chat room. He initially falls ill with a bout of bronchitis and is unable to fullfil his work duties for two weeks. His experience as an online practitioner prompts him to immediately request that the administrator for the course informs his students of the absence by email in conjunction with setting a piece of work to be completed during his absence. The administrator informs the students that Yan will make contact again once recovered. The students are provided with contact details for the co-tutor in the event of needing ad hoc support during this period.

Yan does not make the full recovery from illness in the two weeks as anticipated, and his GP recommends extending his absence by a further four weeks. At this point, it is agreed by Yan, the administrator, and the co-tutor that a referral email be sent out to students explaining that Yan is unable to provide continuing support at this time and is requesting the students' co-operation in being referred to the co-tutor for ongoing academic support and guidance for the remainder of the module.

Although disappointed, the students valued the contact they had received from all parties, as the nature of distance learning had left them feeling more vulnerable during the initial stages of tutor absence than would have been evident if they were studying within the physical location of the university.

Administration of an online practice

Prior to commencing delivery of an online practice, appropriate time and consideration should be devoted to developing administration systems which conform to ethical guidelines. The security of adopted systems should be thoroughly researched prior to their application. A suitable encrypted medium should be sourced to ensure the confidentiality and privacy of the client work and any generated material, in conjunction with password protection for email accounts and any documents which are exchanged.

Prior to launching an online practice, it is essential that practitioners fully consider procedures for the storage and security of data and, where relevant, any therapeutic content generated. Within the UK, such storage is governed by the Data Protection Act 1988; for full information, go to www.ico.gov.uk. It is strongly recommended that practitioners check whether they require Data Controller status in the context of their online practice, or equivalent if their practice is based outside of the UK.

Online practice is very transparent in its nature due to the full content of client interactions being available in a printable format. This places a greater emphasis on a practitioner's responsibility to maintain the confidentiality of client material. This can be achieved by adopting systems which include all personal identifying material being removed from client files during the process of counselling, the sharing of information with third parties such as in supervision, and the storage of client data.

Guidance for preventing unauthorised access to client material   Due to the potentially sensitive nature and volume of material generated when working online with clients, practitioners should be particularly mindful of how they store client work whilst in progress. This includes being alert to ensuring that computers are not accessible or viewable by others whilst engaged in client work or online meetings.

It is advisable to consider including a disclaimer outlining the potential for electronic communication not proving to be 100 per cent reliable or confidential for either party. Within such a disclaimer, it is relevant to include reference to online interactions having an increased potential to be disrupted or cancelled due to technology issues.

Accessibility for clients when accessing an online practitioner resource

Whilst an online practice increases the potential flexibility for clients in gaining access to practitioners, online support may not prove to be an accessible or suitable option for all clients. Online services have a responsibility to realistically form a decision with potential clients as to whether the chosen medium is appropriate, as well as to the practitioner's ability to work with any apparent diversity issues presented by clients.

Where it becomes evident that particular groups of clients are restricted in accessing an online service provision, due to the structure and practicalities of facilities or personal financial resources, it is pertinent to review how the service delivery can be modified to facilitate a more inclusive approach.

Box 8.3 provides an illustration of how effective reviewing of service provision can increase inclusion for clients who are restricted in accessing an existing service.

Box 8.3   Managing the client's restricted access to online services

Neelam is employed by an organisation which is funded by a local authority grant to provide online support to young people who live in the local region. The service is accessed by many young people above the age of 16, but there is a deficit in clients between the ages of 11–16. When reviewing the service users statistics, the organisation draws a conclusion that the younger client group may be disadvantaged due to not being able to secure a private place away from their family members to seek online support.

Neelam's organisation is currently working on a project with the collaboration of local high schools to provide counselling support to students. They decide to carry out a survey amongst students which they hope will identify some of the barriers to this potential client group seeking the option of online support.

The result of the survey indicates that the possible barriers are as they initially anticipated, and with the support of local schools, they decide to research the potential for students to have discrete access to an individual computer suite on an appointment basis where they can secure contact with Neelam and her online colleagues. As a result of this action, the opportunity for younger-aged clients to access online support is enhanced, and the subsequent summary of statistical data analysis confirms this by the number of clients within this age group having increased significantly.

EXERCISE 8.1

DEALING WITH RESTRICTED ACCESS FOR CLIENTS

If you are currently delivering an online practice, consider what steps you are taking or could take to review your systems and service delivery and increase the availability of your service to potential clients who are restricted in accessing the current service provision.

If you are in the process of establishing an online practice, consider what systems you could introduce to develop a broader provision of inclusiveness for potential client groups.

Online client assessment

Assessing suitability of the medium for individual clients   In the course of an online service delivery, there may be instances where assessment conclusions reveal that the available support is not suitable for issues presented by individual clients. Where a formal assessment process is not adopted and clients have open access to practitioners' resources, this may become evident during the course of online contact. Where practitioners engage with clients in professional activities outside of the sphere of therapeutic and mental health services, there may be reduced likelihood of clients presenting in a manner where risk assessment relating to self-harm, or harm to others, may arise. It is still advisable, however, to consider how instances such as this may be responded to.

In the context of mental health, psychiatric, and therapeutic practice, there is a requirement to establish systems in general assessment procedures and an adequate risk assessment system. This provides a safeguard in the event of clients either presenting to a service at risk of harm, or a client moving into an area of risk whilst engaged in online support. Within a face-to-face relationship, the practitioner or service provider has the advantage of physical presence and proximity with clients, which enhances accessibility for referral to local resources where required. The relationship with online clients is more tenuous and therefore provides less scope to be proactive in assisting or referring a client where the need arises. Considerations regarding risk assessment should therefore be included and a clear route identified in the event of this situation arising. Where collaboration in implementing such a procedure is required, it is advisable that guidelines for risk assessment and response have been communicated with all relevant parties within the online service provision.

In reference to duty of care, it is advisable to have emergency contact details available for alternative organisations such as the Samaritans. Such information can be placed on pages of the online practitioner's or organisation's website as a signpost to incoming enquiries from clients requiring additional or emergency support.

Where assessment is a feature of service provision, the following considerations should be integral to adopted systems:

- All assessments are conducted in adherence to ethical guidelines (Suler and Fenichel, 2000).
- Clients should be provided with clear details relating to assessment outcomes and supported in referral to suitable alternative resources.
- In the context of therapeutic practice, it is relevant to conduct a comprehensive assessment process which is ongoing throughout the period of contracted sessions with clients. In circumstances where clients present to a service with a history of enduring mental health difficulties, or is at risk of harm to self or others, online resources and services may not be sufficient to provide support in the context of duty of care. The nature of the physically distanced relationship with online clients may compound this, particularly in situations where a face-to-face alternative cannot be provided within the existing service delivery. Where assessment contra-indicates the potential for a successful outcome, it is important to sensitively offer alternative resources and facilitate onward referral to a relevant and reputable source of support.
- Assessments should include reference to a client's level of competency or confidence in expressing themselves through written words, vocabulary

range, general and emotional expression. Insufficient client aptitude in these areas can increase the potential of misunderstanding by both the practitioner and client to occur. Potential clients may also be limited in their computer literacy and levels of technology skills required for online communication. This should be considered prior to progressing, as communication between the practitioner and client could be adversely affected.

- Where online support is offered to clients as a continuation, or supplementary resource to face-to-face work, it is important to establish with the client whether they have the necessary language articulation and IT competency to make the transition into online working.

Complaints and grievances procedures within an online practice

It is pertinent for practitioners and organisations to have considered how any resulting grievance or complaints from online clients will be responded to and managed. Due to the remote links encountered when engaging with an online practitioner, clients will require reassurances that any resulting grievance or complaint will be responded to appropriately. The manner in which they are convened may differ to that of a face-to-face service, and details relating to procedures should be made available to clients as required. This is a feature of online practice which benefits from the practitioner being affiliated to organisations specialising in this field of practice who can offer both professional guidance and support in such circumstances.

Membership of professional organisations and peer support

Due to the apparent variations in how online practices are structured and delivered, there is an obvious advantage for practitioners in seeking support and guidance from organisations and individual professionals who are specifically focused in this area of service delivery (Evans, 2006; Hanley, 2006).

Affiliation with professional organisations can bring advantages in the following areas:

- Subscribing to defined ethical practice guidelines which offer direction in conducting appropriate professional practice.
- Training and professional development opportunities.
- Support in circumstances where a client wishes to proceed with a formal mediation or complaint process against a practitioner.
- Providing practitioners with opportunities for online discussion forums where professional practice and development themes can be shared and discussed. Such collegial contact can be an invaluable support and information

resource, particularly where practitioners are new to online practice or seeking to share ideas and views on development activities. Such forums offer the opportunity to develop their practice based upon the experiences and expertise of fellow professionals across a diverse range of activities, therefore offering creative solutions to client presenting issues.

- Identifying professional affiliation can reassure clients that the online practitioner is both credible and professional within their service delivery.
- Providing an additional space where practitioners and services can promote themselves to the wider public.
- Practising online is a specialist area and therefore brings its own challenges and rewards. Being affiliated to an organisation specialising in online practice provides the opportunity to remove the sense of isolation which can be apparent within this sphere of professional practice whilst constructing a more prominent voice for this area of professionalism.

Professional affiliation support resources

Within a global context, affiliated professional support is currently available to online practitioners through the following sources:

- www.acto-uk.org: ACTO (Association of Counsellors and Therapists Online) is a UK online organisation which has resources and discussion boards for online counsellors. A group of online therapists formed ACTO in October 2006 because they saw a need for an umbrella organisation in the UK for therapists who practise online. ACTO is a non-profit organisation.
- onlinecounselling@yahoo.co.uk: an online peer practitioner support forum which was established in 2006 and is co-ordinated by Jane Evans.
- www.ismho.org/about.htm: ISMHO (International Society for Mental Health Online) was formed in 1997 to promote the understanding, use, and development of online communication, information, and technology for the international mental health community. ISMHO is a non-profit organisation.

Supervision arrangements for online practitioners

For some professionals, the supervision of client work will not be a requirement, whilst for others this will be an ongoing feature within their occupational framework. Variations in the definition of supervision will also be evident and influenced by the context of work conducted. The traditional medium for receiving direction and support with client work is based in face-to-face meetings with a supervisor or peers as a process of developing skills and knowledge, in conjunction with monitoring efficacy in client work and adherence to ethical and professional guidelines. The opportunity to engage in supervision through an online medium may feel alien to those practitioners who have little or no knowledge of the manner in which this is conducted and the potential benefits it offers. One of the distinct benefits of accessing online supervision is both parties having a full text-based record of material generated from the supervision exchange (Stokes, 2006).

To date, there are limited resources which refer to the characteristics of online supervision, the manner in which this is organised and facilitated, and the benefits to professional practice. The conclusion of this section serves to increase awareness of and interest in the benefits in this area of support available to practitioners.

Clinical supervision

Where supervision is a feature for an online practitioner, the supervisor should be competent and experienced to a degree where they can offer appropriate support and guidance which is specific to this field of practice, particularly so when a practitioner is developing skills whilst engaging online with clients.

Therapeutic contexts

It is strongly recommended that online counsellors receive clinical supervision or clinical support from professionals who are fully familiar with the medium and the potential implications of the work with clients. The variations and additional skill requirements an online practitioner will need to draw upon in order to practise ethically and professionally with clients cannot be fulfilled by a supervisor who has limited or no clinical experience and understanding of the specific issues in this work.

General support and guidance contexts

Where practitioners are adopting the use of online counselling skills as a new addition to their professional practice, it is strongly recommended that professional support or peer supervision is sought to assist in the process of meeting service delivery, in conjunction with any ethical and legal requirements specific to their online practice such as those identified throughout this book.

Box 8.4 and Box 8.5 provide simulated illustrations of the format and rationale for seeking online supervision in a variety of contexts.

Box 8.4   The benefits of a supervisor experienced in online practice

Petra works online with clients as an extension to her private face-to-face therapeutic practice. She receives clinical supervision for this work on a monthly basis, and visits the supervisor for this service. Petra's supervisor has no experience or training relating to working online with clients, and although he could support her to some degree on aspects of the therapeutic work, he feels unable to empathise with the relational and further-reaching aspects of Petra's work.

Petra decided prior to developing her online practice that she would seek the support of an online supervisor. She meets with her online supervisor twice monthly through a combination of email and synchronous exchanges, also having the opportunity of back-up via telephone contact if required. One example of Petra valuing this medium of supervision support arose with a client who was sporadic in her contact and seemed unwilling to engage in regular ongoing appointments. The client then ended sessions without notice, but returned some months later requesting further support. Petra had become accustomed to a situation within her face-to-face counselling work where the majority of her clients were consistent and arrived for appointments on time for weekly appointments. If they were intending to end therapy, there was usually a planned process which clients engaged with. Petra was finding that her irritation with the online client, caused by frequently 'arriving' late for appointments or cancelling at short notice, was affecting her ability to offer unconditional positive regard to the client. She decided to take this issue to supervision with the intent of identifying boundaries which could help with responding to clients who presented in this manner, whilst also seeking to improve the dynamics in the relationship with the identified client. The supervisor had experienced such occurrences within her own online practice and was able to share her approach in responding to clients and online boundaries with Petra.

A brief summary of the supervisor's questions included the following:

- Was Petra anticipating that online clients should fit into a similar routine as her face-to-face clients, that is regular weekly appointments, and would Petra want to consider introducing a system of flexible arrangement for clients who couldn't commit to weekly sessions?
- What workable boundaries might Petra be able to put in place when clients presented in this manner?

- Had Petra communicated to her client the relevance and benefits of endings, even when temporarily ceasing contact for a brief period?
- What dynamics may be evident in that particular client example which may have contributed to the client being resistant to engaging in regular sessions with an appropriate ending?

The benefits to Petra in taking this matter to supervision featured predominantly in the guidance and support she received from a supervisor who was familiar with the dynamics of how this was impacting on the client work and Petra herself, and assisted the supervisee in establishing ways to respond effectively to the current client issues.

EXERCISE 8.2

FLEXIBILITY IN AN ONLINE RELATIONSHIP

Given the case study example in Box 8.4, consider how you might approach, or do currently approach, the situation with online clients where they request flexibility in their appointment schedule, in addition to displaying a reluctance on their part to commit to an agreed ending.

Having defined or reviewed the current procedure for flexible working arrangements, consider how this can be effectively communicated and agreed with clients so that both parties achieve a workable and professionally structured online relationship.

Box 8.5   The need for dedicated professional support

Simon is a voluntary worker with an online organisation which provides a variety of resources for individuals and couples seeking support with relationship and marriage issues, including an online forum where clients make asynchronous contributions to discussion topics. Simon's duties include moderating online forum entries and responding to replies where 'expert' guidance is sought from individual members. He has the opportunity of peer support when

(Continued)

(Continued)

encountering issues which require discussion prior to posting a response, and the service manager is sometimes available to discuss his work.

Simon feels that dedicated supervision with a professional who is experienced in managing forums and discussion boards, whilst also not employed by the organisation, would be valuable to both his work and professional development. The current support available to Simon is structured in a way that does not provide access to consultation as and when required. Often colleagues and the service manager are required to find space within their own work commitments to talk with Simon regarding client issues. The basis of the current support is also face-to-face and does not reflect the medium in which he engages with clients.

EXERCISE   8.3

DEDICATED PROFESSIONAL SUPPORT

In the light of Box 8.5, what do you consider to be the potential benefits and drawbacks in Simon receiving dedicated, individual professional support with a supervisor who is both experienced in this field of online practice and works independently from the organisation?

How might Simon present a case to the service manager to request funding for supervision support with his online practice?

The two examples within Box 8.4 and Box 8.5 provide a brief insight to the potential benefits of specific supervision which is provided by a professional who has insight to the features of online practice. There are distinct advantages in receiving supervision through an online source as this provides an opportunity for the practitioner to enhance their skills and technology awareness and aptitude, whilst providing a platform where they can increase the level of empathy with clients who seek support through an online medium.

Summary

There are many implications which can affect and impact upon the quality of service which clients receive when engaging in an online relationship with professionals. It is the responsibility of practitioners to ensure that they have appropriately planned and deliver their client services within an ethical and legal framework which neither compromises themselves nor the clients they interact with. The subject matter within this chapter and the examples highlighting good practice, in conjunction with practical exercises and points for further consideration, provide a solid platform for ensuring the required level of service delivery to clients. Such guidance and activities are relevant across the broad spectrum of professional fields where practitioners engage with clients through computer-mediated technology.

I have highlighted the many benefits in seeking affiliation to professional organisations who support online practitioners, which is particularly pertinent within a relatively new and developing context of engaging with service users. The introduction of a regulation or screening facility to provide reassurances to clients in the efficacy of practitioners they engage with is a matter which requires attention by regulatory bodies (Pergament, 1998).

Supervision may not be a resource which all readers of this book are familiar with, and I hope that the manner in which it has been introduced in this chapter provides an opportunity to consider the potential benefits to those who establish an online presence with clients.

Points for consideration

- What systems would you consider appropriate to your own area of specialism in circumstances where a practitioner is unable to fulfil appointment obligations with clients due to ill health, or instances of extended absence?
- Within the considerations of assessment and risk management, what is the identified format for 'duty of care' to service users within your sphere of professional practice and the requirements within the specific context of the organisation that employs you as an online practitioner? How does this define the structure of delivery of service to clients, and any resulting influences on your relationship, or potential relationship, with online clients?
- What systems do you have in place to assess and risk-manage your current practice with clients, and how does this transfer into online practice with clients?
- In the context of professional affiliation support, what would you consider to be the advantages to you of reinforcing the professionalism of your work by either joining an existing organisation allied to your field of practice, or alternatively establishing an online forum where you invite other colleagues to work collaboratively with you?
- If you were ever to receive a complaint or grievance within your sphere of professional online practice, what systems of support do you have at hand with responding and managing the process? In addition, do you have appropriate insurance cover for such incidences, and what process would be required by your insurer?

References

ACA (American Counselling Association) (2007) *Code of Ethics: As Approved by the ACA Governing Council 2005.* Available at www.counselling.org/Resources/ CodeOfEthics/TP/Home/CT2.aspx.

Ainsworth, M. et al (2000) Suggested Principles for the Online Provision of Mental Health Services, version 3.11. Available at http://www.ismho.org/builder/?p=page &id=214.

BACP/Anthony, K. and Jamieson, A. (2005) *Guidelines for Counseling and Psychotherapy*, 2nd edition. Lutterworth: BACP. p. 9.

Guterman, J.T. and Kirk, M.A. (1999) 'Mental health counselors and the Internet', *Journal of Mental Health Counseling*, 21 (4): 309–25.

Evans, J. (2006) 'Student support – new directions; online counselling service,' *AUCC Journal*, winter edition. Available at www.aucc.uk.com/journal_pdf/winter06_5.pdf.

Evans, J. (2007) 'A pullout guide to online counseling and psychotherapy in universities and colleges', *AUCC Journal*, December.

Halpern, L. (2007) *Online Services for Students*. Lutterworth: Association for University and College Counselling Publications. Available at www.aucc.uk.com/ pubs.html.

Hanley, T. (2006) 'Student support – new directions; online student support', *AUCC Journal*, December. Available at www.aucc.uk.com/journal_pdf/winter06_4.pdf.

NBCC (2007a) *The Practice of Internet Counseling: Standards for The Ethics of Internet Counseling*. Greensboro, NC: National Board for Certified Counselors and Center for Credentialising and Education. Available at www.nbcc.org/webethics2.

NBCC (2007b) *Legal Considerations, Licensure, and Certification: The Practice of Internet Counselling*. Greenboro, NC: National Board for Certified Counselors and Center for Credentialising and Education. Available at www.nbcc.org/webethics2.

Pergament, D. (1998) 'Health matrix', *Journal of Law Medicine*, 8 (2): 233–79.

Stokes, A. (2006) *Supervision in Cyberspace*. Available at www.counsellingatwork. org.uk/journal_pdf/acw_winter06_b.pdf.

Suler, J. and Fenichel, M. (2000) *Assessing a Person's Suitability for Online Therapy: Clinical Case Study Group Findings*. International Society for Mental Health Online. Available at www.ismho.org/builder//?p=page&id=222.

Trepal, H., Haberstroh, S., Duffey, T. and Evans, M. (2007) 'Considerations and stratgies for teaching online counseling skills: establishing a relationship in cyberspace', *Counselor Education & Supervision*, 46 (June).

CONCLUSION

There were many aspects that I would like to have discussed within the conclusion of this book, in the anticipation that I might promote further consideration and encouragement to readers on the subject of online counselling and guidance skills. However, I've had to limit both my enthusiasm for the subject and the content presented to focus on points that I hope will provide further insight to readers on how they might engage with the current and future developments in this field of practice. I have also included some 'food for thought' on the immediate issues applicable to the process of promoting a wider understanding, and the apparent significance of computer-mediated engagement with clients.

Computer-mediated technology as a viable resource and support for clients

'Ask uncle Ezra', the world's first online advice column, was launched in 1986 and is the earliest recorded instance of a computer-mediated client resource. It was established by Cornell University as a support facility for their student population. Issues relating to confidentiality may be a contributing factor in the noticeable limitations when seeking to establish the extent of additional areas of activity, either prior to or subsequent to this point in time. Due to the evident restrictions in publicising client activity and engagement with such resources, this may limit aspects of research data that could assist in ascertaining the many variations and outcomes of service delivery where computer-mediated technology has been adopted to sustain supportive practitioner and client relationships. It is highly likely that, from an historical perspective, all fields of professional activity where practitioners provide supportive interaction to clients in a face-to-face context have utilised computer-mediated resources at varying stages to communicate and sustain contact with potential or actual clients. This may have included email, with such contact being informal or ad hoc, and based upon convenience to both parties in the process of maintaining engagement, or providing information, in between face-to-face meetings. Without doubt, the resulting outcomes from both formal and informal computer-mediated client and practitioner exchanges will have contributed to the current developments where computer-mediated resources are deployed as a vehicle for providing client services. At the point of concluding research for their book, Marks et al. (2007) had identified up to 100 differing computer-mediated treatment packages in use across a global context, whilst also forecasting a continuing increase in developments and application in such resources. This feature of practitioner support and guidance, in conjunction with self-help guided programmes, is stated as being significant to successful client outcomes.

During the writing of this chapter, I conducted an Internet search using the key words 'online counselling, guidance, and support'. This produced 1,950,000 associated results. The willingness for clients to engage with practitioners using computer-mediated communication, either on a formal or informal basis, has to be acknowledged as reinforcement to the relevance and potential for this to fulfil a significant niche in the wide range of supportive resources available at this time, and also within future advancements in this field. Smith (2005) discusses a Canadian computer-mediated support service for young people called 'Ask a Counsellor', where postings have increased from 74 to 2,267 per month during the 12-month period between February 2004 to March 2005. Female postings outnumbered those by males on a 4:1 ratio.

There may be some professionals or 'observers' of this relatively new and developing field of practice who might argue that clients are actively engaging with computer-mediated supportive services where their needs could be more aptly met within the more traditional scope of face-to-face practice. It is not my intention here to attempt to dismiss or allay concerns and reservations that others may hold regarding the viability and professionalism in this area of supportive practice. I consider the content of the book has provided thought and guidance on how such concerns can be addressed in the process of securing a professional and ethical service for clients. I hope that the simulated case study material and exercises included with each chapter have provided readers with insightful opportunities to attain greater understanding of the value of supporting clients in this manner and the necessary skills required to achieve this. I would also like to emphasise that I do not envisage that engaging with clients in this manner holds a higher regard or will supersede the relevance and benefits of face-to-face engagement with clients. Nonetheless, I would hope that online support can achieve its relevant place in being a recognised and valued resource for supporting clients and service users.

The advent of the Internet and the development of computer-mediated technology and resources will continue to be a feature which holds the potential to influence how individuals form supportive interactions across a global canvas. Professionals have a choice in how and at what level they choose to engage in such developments. The continuing points of consideration throughout future developments in this area will be a requirement for those practitioners and organisations that do elect to provide computer-mediated resources for clients, to ensure their compliance with professional, legal, and ethical guidelines, whilst also demonstrating a commitment to continuous review regarding the maintenance and improvement of their service delivery.

The relevance of research

The field of research, using randomised control groups and contexts of service delivery, will no doubt prove to highlight areas where computer-mediated outcomes and appropriate service delivery are proving to meet client needs, whilst also conforming to the requirements of legal, ethical and professional boundaries. Amongst others, the specialised field of computer-mediated treatment programmes is an area where research evidence is being undertaken and providing some insight to the potential benefits for clients (Marks et al., 2007). An overriding outcome from such research indicates that there is difficulty in defining whether these are more beneficial than other traditional forms of treatment, as the emphasis lies in what works best for each individual, the presenting issues, and their circumstances, as opposed to generalised outcomes. This may be similar to the dilemma where research has sought to identify which of all available modalities of face-to-face counselling and psychotherapy hold the potential for greater client outcomes. There is always the feature of individual client needs and differences which affect how a client engages with such evident variation in theoretical approaches and in turn influences the resulting outcomes. An additional consideration, in either a face-to-face or alternative context, is how effectively a client engages with their practitioner. Within computer-mediated supportive and therapeutic interventions, a significant factor in determining the potential for successful client outcomes lies in a client's willingness and ability to engage with a practitioner and the specific intent of the service delivery.

Currently, there are a range of guidelines which indicate what specific client issues and presenting mental health features would be considered as unsuitable for therapeutic support or treatment using computer-mediated technology (Anthony and Jamieson, 2005; ISMHO, 2000; Suler, 2000). There may be distinct benefits for other fields of computer-mediated professional practice, where issues relating to mental health and supportive interactions feature within their client relationships, to identify criteria for establishing suitability of this media for their client groups. As growth in this field of practice progresses, there is a requirement for continuous review and research in this area.

At present, there is a dramatic increase and diverse range of service providers who are seeking to engage clients through this medium. As would be apparent in face-to-face service provision, it is pertinent for individuals and organisations to include the feature of continuous research and evaluation within the short- and longer-term structure and planning of these resources. The inclusion of such features will:

- assist in securing a platform for benchmarking and regulation in all manners of computer-mediated client resources
- assist in ascertaining the effectiveness of computer-mediated client support within a diverse range of service delivery contexts

- provide reliable and consistent sources of research which influence future development activities in this field of practice
- serve to improve the overall standards of service delivery across the spectrum of computer-mediated client support
- assist in clarifying aspects of service structure, client outcomes, and so on, which in turn may serve to allay areas of the apparent anxiety and scepticism regarding the relevance and future scope within this context of client support
- provide the potential for clients to express their opinions regarding the efficacy and professional viability of computer-mediated support, in conjunction with providing a voice for clients in the forging of future developments. This will be particularly relevant in areas where specific client groups have been under-represented within traditional forms of face-to-face supportive relationships, yet have found inclusion through computer-mediated technology resources
- provide an opportunity to continuously monitor and review the nature of client presenting issues which can be appropriately supported by adopting the use of computer-mediated software and technology.

An example of how research might provide greater insight to the benefits/disadvantages of computer-mediated relationships with clients

There is considerable material available which refers to the potential dynamics that are initiated within computer-mediated relationships. The following points highlight where appropriate research may assist in providing insight to such influences and the resulting outcomes.

Suler (2004) identifies the aspect of visual cues being absent within text-only communication as a point of criticism from those who believe this form of communication induces an ambiguous and depleted relationship. The absence of visual and physical characteristics is proposed as a distinct advantage due to the potential for clients to engage with practitioners without aspects of transference dynamics which may be evident within face-to-face exchanges. This may therefore provide opportunities for individuals to be released from preoccupations relating to gender, race, culture, general appearance, and so on. Thus, this offers a unique occasion for individuals to experience a release from personal factors and inhibitions which induce a negative impact in other areas of their life, including participation in study, when seeking support or therapeutic assistance, within business or personal relationships, and so on.

From an opposing viewpoint, this may not be evident in all instances, and the absence of a client's physical presence may restrict a practitioner's ability to secure the desired levels of empathy. An online practitioner colleague has consented to my inclusion of their encountering an asynchronous online client where aspects of negative transference had impacted upon them being able to secure the desired level of empathy. When the client subsequently approached the counselling service for face-to-face support after a few months from completion of their computer-mediated exchanges, the client was offered the opportunity to meet with the same practitioner or an alternative face-to-face counsellor: the client elected to meet with their former online counsellor due to feeling that they were already familiar with the presenting issues. The previous transference responses were not apparent during the face-to-face meeting, and this resulted in the practitioner experiencing a more enhanced and positive empathy with the client and their presenting issues.

Training and additional opportunities for the sharing of good practice for those professionals engaged in computer-mediated supportive relationships with clients

At the time of writing, there were limited training opportunities for practitioners that offered guidance relating to engaging with client groups using computer-mediated technology. Where available, the training content does not encompass the full diversity of circumstances and professional duties where practitioners currently engage with clients and the specific considerations which are pertinent to each. There would be distinct advantages in a broader range of training opportunities being made available, including the inclusion of a specific focus and direction for practitioners on the technology forms which will be adopted within the intended client practice (Kraus et al., 2004). It would be considered inappropriate for face-to-face practitioners to have acquired certificated competency as an endorsement for engaging with clients without having undertaken training and assessment in face-to-face training activities. Equally, the nature of distance engagement with clients should be reflected by training programmes for online practitioners holding a strong emphasis on remote learning activities (Anthony and Jamieson, 2005).

Case discussion groups and peer support forums are a valued resource within the field of therapeutic computer-mediated client practice. Such arenas exemplify the sharing of good practice and provide support for new areas of development. All practitioners who engage with clients, regardless of specialism, may benefit from developing or participating in such activities, as they hold the potential to provide an equally valid and worthwhile experience. I have previously referred to the potential benefits in securing affiliation to professional organisations that offer support to online practitioners within their area of specialism. At the time of writing, there are a number of such organisations who provide a service to online therapeutic and mental health practitioners, but there is a deficit of resources available to those practitioners engaged in activities with clients outside of this remit. This is a matter which, if addressed, could enhance the support and guidance for practitioners across a broad canvas of computer-mediated client activities.

There is a requirement for those who oversee the professional standards of practitioners across the range of professional occupations, where there is movement towards engaging with clients using computer-mediated technologies, to encourage the introduction of forums where specific considerations can be discussed and offer guidance which is specific to practitioners' field of practice.

I find it encouraging that there is evidence to support a developing awareness of counsellor training programmes realising the significance in encouraging students to learn and conduct research into the subject of online counselling and supervision. Within the last year, I have frequently received email requests, via my website, where face-to-face counselling students have been directed by tutors to seek information or brief interviews where practitioners provide insight into their professional online counselling or supervision practice.

Attitudes of society towards computer-mediated engagement with clients

It is logical to acknowledge that there may be evidence of caution on behalf of some members of society regarding the potential for online and computer-mediated activity with clients to provide appropriate care, service level requirements, and outcomes. There are frequent publicised accounts of the Internet introducing an arena where charlatans establish themselves in online practice and compromise the well-being and financial resources of individuals, groups, and organisations. Prior to and in conjunction with the advent of the Internet, there is evidence of reports where similar activity has occurred within face-to-face engagement with service providers. The increased wariness or scepticism regarding adopting the use of computer-based technologies may lie in individuals holding the belief that face-to-face encounters provide additional reassurances due to being based in a physical locality with the service provider. Computer-mediated supportive interactions cannot offer the same reassurances. This book has provided discussion in areas where practitioners can seek to enhance the scope for clients to gain a sense of the validity and professionalism of their service, whilst also offering guidance relating to the provision of continuous features of reassurance in the form of explicit contracting and service guidelines, and adopting the use of secure and encrypted communication facilities, data storage, and so on.

The attitudes of society will form an important aspect of computer mediated approaches to client support achieving increased credibility and value. The securing of such a position places responsibility upon individual practitioners to conduct their practice in a manner that promotes confidence in all areas of their professional activities, but also calls upon professional bodies and organisations aligned to all facets within this field of practice to:

- actively encourage research projects which assist in gaining insight and understanding of the advantages and drawbacks of supporting clients using computer-mediated technology
- increase the instances where practitioners are actively encouraged to submit articles for professional journals and provide insight to their online activities with clients
- encourage the development of focused training opportunities which are allied to specific areas of online practitioner specialisms
- support existing training providers to include modules relating to computer-mediated supportive relationships with clients where there is the likelihood of this subject featuring within practitioners' fields of practice
- promote opportunities for focus groups to explore the potential for developing or introducing a broader range of diversification within computer-mediated resources and facilities for clients.

Consideration to the potential for computer-mediated supportive relationships to harmoniously sit alongside face-to-face services

Discussions and research relating to the effectiveness and place of computer-mediated supportive relationships will no doubt continue far beyond the publication of this book. Currently, there is continuing debate relating to computer-mediated client support being able to firmly secure a place where it is valued and acknowledged as credible within its own right, and find appropriate acceptance in relation to face-to-face alternatives.

In addition to the lack of research evidence to promote greater understanding of the potential for computer-mediated support and therapeutic interventions to hold its place alongside face-to-face practice, there may also be a lack of understanding and interest from practitioners and professional bodies regarding the value within this field of specialism. There is also the possibility that elements of resistance may emanate from individuals not holding sufficient confidence to utilise computer-mediated technology within their client practice, whilst also anticipating that aspects of them as unique individuals may be lost during computer-mediated exchanges with clients. Currently, I deploy the use of counselling skills within both face-to-face and computer-mediated therapeutic interventions with clients. I also use these skills in both contexts when participating and facilitating forums, training programmes, case discussion groups, or conversing through email exchanges, and so on. I value the benefits, dynamics, and the potential available within both perspectives. Each hold specific values relating to the focus of the interaction and desired outcomes. I regularly receive email contact from clients who openly express that they have chosen online counselling due to feeling inhibited in disclosing the nature of their presenting issues within face-to-face therapeutic support, or who wish to 'test the water' in this manner prior to considering approaching a face-to-face service. Many of the presenting issues are related to shame and guilt inhibitors. Online supportive interactions can provide a platform to discuss such feelings and related experiences in a manner that may not be evident when meeting a practitioner within face-to-face exchanges.

It is pertinent to consider that a combination of face-to-face and computer-mediated exchanges could have a significant impact upon the overall content and outcomes of practitioners' engagement with individual clients. This would form a very interesting and insightful basis for research activity.

Computer-mediated supportive exchanges as a tool for increasing access for clients with disabilities or geographical and personal restricting influences

I consider it relevant to conclude this chapter by reiterating points made throughout this book which refer to the potential benefits that computer-mediated services and technologies can offer in assisting those clients who are restricted in securing access to face-to-face services. There are wide ranges of contributing factors which result in individuals and groups across a global canvas being excluded from supportive engagement with practitioners. This is often due to many factors which can be alleviated by organisations offering alternative features, including computer-mediated resources. A brief summary of such restricting factors includes:

- The geographical location of clients and available services within their locality.
- Health and physical mobility restricting influences which prevent the potential to access face-to-face services.
- Within higher and further education organisations, students may be engaged in distance learning or placement activity which restricts access to face-to-face service provision.
- Within the area of employment, individuals may be deployed to locations or countries where suitable face-to-face services are unavailable. Language barriers may also be a significant inhibiting factor within such circumstances.
- Individual personal and work schedules may prevent opportunities to engage with routine support services as these are not usually available beyond limited opening hours.

- Clients who suffer with anxiety or phobia-based disorders may be unable to consider approaching routine and therapeutic face-to-face support services.
- There may be restrictions on potential clients being able to seek support from face-to-face services due to their age or physical/mental health issues. Such issues may prevent or inhibit opportunities to leave the home unaccompanied. This may be particularly pertinent to young people and adolescents, dementia sufferers, and so on.
- Fear of stigmatisation.
- Cultural, gender, sexuality issues, and so on which may influence an individual in being able to consider approaching face to face support.
- In locations where clients are members of a close-knit community, there may be an internalised or explicit rationale for electing not to access locally based support networks due to an anticipated negative response if others became aware of their engagement with a service provision.

This list is not exhaustive, but does offer insight to areas where potential clients are restricted in accessing support due to variations within their personal circumstances and external influences. It is therefore relevant for organisations to consider how they might introduce a wider inclusion for those clients who are unable to secure or are restricted in securing support and resources which are currently only available via face-to-face exchanges with practitioners.

I hope that the variety of discussion subjects within this book have offered readers the opportunity to reflect upon their existing online or computer-mediated practice with clients, whilst also serving to encourage those practitioners who are considering adapting their existing face-to-face counselling and guidance skills into a position where they proceed to engage with clients in this manner. Part II has focused on supporting practitioners in the professional, legal, and ethical issues which are apparent within this field of practice, and I anticipate that the subject matter discussed may provide material which serves as a continuing reference point in the planning stages and conducting of supportive activities with clients.

References

Anthony, K. and Jamieson, A. (2005) *Guidelines for Online Counselling and Psychotherapy*, 2nd edition. Lutterworth: British Association for Counselling and Psychotherapy. p. 4.

ISMHO (2000) *Assessing a Person's Suitability for Online Therapy*. Available at www.ismho.org/builder//?p page&id 222.

Kraus, R., Zack, J. and Stricker, G. (2004) *Online Counselling: A Handbook for Mental Health Practitioners*. London: Elsevier/Academic Press. p. 95.

Marks, I.M., Cavanagh, K. and Gega, L. (2007) *Hands-on-Help: Computer Aided Psychotherapy*. Maudsley Monographs, no 49. Hove: Psychology Press.

Smith, E. (2005) *Online Counselling Comes of Age: Young People being Drawn to Use Web-based Facility due to Anonymity*. News @OFT. Toronto: Social Sciences, Business and Law, University of Toronto. Available at www.news.utoronto.ca/bin6/051011-1731.asp.

Suler, J. (2000) *Ethics in Cyberspace Research*. Available at http://www.usnrider.edu/~suler/psycyber/ethics.html.

Suler, J. (2004) *Psychology of Cyberspace: In-Person versus Cyberspace Relationships*. Available at users.rider.edu/~suler/psycyber/showdown.html.

INDEX

Research Methods Books
from SAGE

Basics of
QUALITATIVE
RESEARCH
3e

Juliet Corbin
Anselm Strauss

The
Mixed
Methods
Reader

Vicki L. Plano Clark • John W. Creswell

DOING
QUALITATIVE
RESEARCH
USING
YOUR COMPUTER

A PRACTICAL GUIDE

CHRIS HAHN

SECOND EDITION
INTERVIEWS
Learning the Craft of Qualitative Research Interviewing

Steinar Kvale
Svend Brinkmann

DISCOVERING STATISTICS
USING SPSS THIRD EDITION

ANDY FIELD

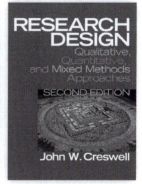
RESEARCH
DESIGN
Qualitative,
Quantitative,
and Mixed Methods
Approaches
SECOND EDITION

John W. Creswell

www.sagepub.co.uk

The Qualitative Research Kit

Edited by Uwe Flick

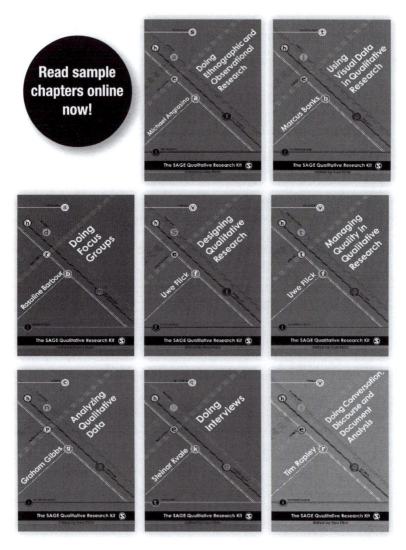

www.sagepub.co.uk

Printed in Poland
by Amazon Fulfillment
Poland Sp. z o.o., Wrocław